ABSTRACT OF FOUR LECTURES ON BUDDHIST LITERATURE IN CHINA

ABSTRACT OF FOUR LECTURES ON

BUDDHIST LITERATURE IN CHINA

SAMUEL BEAL

GYAN

Published by

Gyan Publishing House
5, Ansari Road
Daryaganj, New Delhi-110002
Phone: 011-47034999, 9811692060
E-mail: books@gyanbooks.com

Distribution Network
gyanbooks.com
India, USA, Canada, UK, Australia, France

ISBN : 978-81-212-3185-5 (PB)
First Published, London, 1882

2nd Impression 2020

Printed at: Gyan Press, Delhi.

ABSTRACT OF FOUR LECTURES

ON

BUDDHIST LITERATURE IN CHINA

DELIVERED AT

UNIVERSITY COLLEGE, LONDON.

BY

SAMUEL BEAL,

PROFESSOR OF CHINESE, UNIV. COLL. LOND.

LONDON:

TRÜBNER & CO., LUDGATE HILL.

1882.

山越弥陀

TO

GEORGE CRAWSHAY, ESQ.,

OF HAUGHTON CASTLE, NORTHUMBERLAND,

HIMSELF A STUDENT OF BUDDHISM AND AN ADEPT IN CHINESE LITERATURE,

I DEDICATE

This Little Book,

AS A TRIBUTE OF ESTEEM AND FRIENDSHIP.

INTRODUCTION.

In the introduction to a work[1] published in the year 1871 I called attention to the fact that we possessed at that time, in England at least, no complete set of the Buddhist Sacred Writings as they are known in China and Japan. These Sacred Writings, constituting what is called the Tripiṭaka, or three receptacles, had been printed at various times in China from wooden blocks, which were as often destroyed by fire or civil war. It is said that during the Sung and Yüan dynasties (A.D. 960–1330) as many as twenty different editions had been produced, but during the troubles occurring towards the end of the Yüan period all these perished. During the Ming dynasty (A.D. 1360–1620) two editions, called the Southern and the Northern, were published, the latter of which was reproduced in 1586 by a priest called Mi-tsang, after twenty years' labour. This edition is known in Japan as the Ming tsong, or Tripiṭaka of the Ming dynasty.

It is this copy of the Sacred Books that I requested His Excellency Iwakura Tomomi to procure for the India Office Library, and which he so generously promised to do, in 1874. A similar request had been already made at Pekin, but the Chinese Government, jealously conservative, had declined to accede to it. We were fortunately able to look elsewhere; and in 1875 the entire Tripiṭaka was received at the India Office, in fulfilment of the promise made by the Japanese ambassador.

Lest these books should remain on the library shelves unexamined and uncared for, I thought they might provide

[1] Catena of Buddhist Scriptures, from the Chinese.

me with material for a course of lectures I had undertaken to deliver at University College, London, on the subject of Buddhist literature in China. Accordingly, having prepared a catalogue of the books, imperfect indeed, but sufficient for practical purposes, I proceeded to examine some of them more attentively. The result of my inquiries I embodied in the lectures I delivered during the years 1879–1880, and I have in the following pages printed an abstract of these, with a view to call attention to the subject.

I thought, first of all, it would be interesting to recount the names and the labours of those Indian, or at any rate foreign, Buddhist priests, who during 600 years and more after the beginning of the Christian era continued to arrive in China with books and manuscripts, which they subsequently translated, or assisted to translate, into the language of that country. It is surely an interesting study to inquire how these foreign priests succeeded in converting China to Buddhism. If they had failed, yet the exhibition of this fresh energy in the world—this energy, I mean, of religious propagandism—would naturally excite some curiosity. We should be inclined to ask whether it was derived from the genius of the Buddhist religion, or whether it was but a widened circle of an energy excited from another centre. And if it could be shown that it was an independent movement, we should be led to inquire further how far it was confined in its direction, and why so. But, apart from this, we have in the fact of the rapid spread of the Buddhist belief throughout the eastern portion of Asia a study sufficient for the present at least. The mere record of names would be of itself useless if it did not convey the idea of earnest and persevering work. And it is for the purpose of calling attention to the reality of this work that I have recited the names of some of the Buddhist priests who came to China and worked there, teaching and translating, during the first six centuries of our era. With respect to the character of their work, it would be surely enough to point to results. A new literature was produced—a literature essentially Indian, and therefore Aryan; the Chinese were inspired with new thoughts and ideas about religion; a rude blow was dealt to their national exclusiveness, another turn was given to their studies, and fresh combinations of men and women formed into religious societies; the country was covered with temples and pagodas; and thousands, stirred by this new impulse, sought to find out in the solitude of the hermit's cell the secret of the unrest that had seized them.

The Buddhists of India brought about all this, and much more than this; for what occurred in China happened also throughout the regions beyond; and in due course Corea, Japan, on that side, and Mongolia and Tibet on the other, were converted and made obedient to the same faith, or whatever it was in Buddhism, that had conquered the Eastern world.

But my task is not to exhibit the mode or even the character of this change, but to call attention to the fact and the steps which led to it.

No doubt one cause of the rapid spread of Buddhism northward from the valley of the Ganges is to be found in the existence of a Northern people, the Vajjis or Samvajjis, in the neighbourhood of Magadha, where this religion was first preached. It is a curious discovery to find that a republic, so to speak, of Northern invaders, the Yue-chi of Chinese history, were already settled in India when Buddha lived, and were converted to his doctrine by his own instrumentality. Yet such is the case. We arrive at it in this way. The Vajjians, who lived in Vesâli and some other neighbouring towns, are denoted in Chinese by the same symbols as are used to describe the Yue-chi. Mr. Rhys Davids, in his Buddhist Suttas[1] (chap. i. § 3), gives a translation relating to the Vajjians, which I had already translated as referring to the Yue-chi (Fa-kheu-pi-u, pp. 165 and 166); and M. Léon Féer, in his translation of the Sûtra of Forty-two Articles, had noticed that the Getæ (Yue-chi), in my translation of the same book, ought to be restored to Vrijjis. This was sufficient to show that the symbols employed by the Chinese to denote the Northern people, who are in fact the White Huns or Viddhals of history, are also employed to denote the Vajjis of Vesâli. But the

[1] Sacred Books of the East, vol. xi.

Vajjis are also called Litsavis or Litchavis, and these again Mr. Brian Hodgson (Essays, p. 17 *n.*) had identified with the Scyths. On turning again to Mr. Fergusson's "Tree and Serpent Worship" (pl. xxviii. fig. 1, and text), I was glad to be able to identify the people here drawn as the inhabitants of Vesâli. For this worshipping of the Tope is, in fact, the dedication feast of the Vajjians after they had obtained a share of Buddha's relics. This will be plain from observing that all the scenes connected with it, viz., those on the inside of the right-hand pillar of the Northern gateway, relate to events which happened at Vesâli. The group given on pl. xvi. fig. 2 (*op. cit.*) is found immediately beneath it, and is a view of the monkeys bringing a pot of honey to Buddha near the Markaṭahrada at Vesâli, as related in Hiouen Thsang (ii. 387). Beneath this again is the scene describing Mâra's interview with Buddha, when he exhorted him to leave the world (Jul. ii. 391). This is plain from the marked presence of the women (his daughters), who take such a conspicuous part in the Buddhist temptation-scene. In the same group (pl. xxvi. fig. 1) is the representation of the Kinnaras who followed Buddha when he was going to the scene of his death at Kusinagara, as related by Hiouen Thsang (Jul. ii. 390). The perfect agreement of these plates with Hiouen Thsang's account of what he heard (or what was believed) at Vesâli, seems to prove that this portion of the pillar was finished at the expense of the Vajjian Buddhists. Now Mr. Fergusson had already commented on the strange appearance of the worshippers in the upper group (pl. xxviii. fig. 1). He says (p. 136), "These people are not Hindus, but an entirely different race, who are seen at Sanchi only in this bas-relief. Their hair is short and curly like a negro's, or as that of Buddha is represented to be in more modern times. . . . The Roman double pipe replaces the flute. The trumpets are of a kind seen nowhere else in the sculptures, but are almost identical with those represented on the arch at Orange and elsewhere by the Romans as belonging to the Celts or their barbarian enemies, whoever they were. Their banner alone, with 'stars and stripes,' or rather stars and Union Jack combined, is like what we shall afterwards meet." I assume that Mr. Fergusson, in this last clause, refers to the same flag as we see it pl. xxxviii. fig. 1. Now this scene undoubtedly refers to the siege of Kusinagara by the allied troops, who represented the various states (seven) that demanded a share of Buddha's relics. This siege is fully narrated in Asvaghosha's *Buddhacharita*, and also in the *Lalita Vistara* (Foucaux's translation, p. 424). The Vajjians took part in it; this flag therefore is the Vajjian flag. Now all this is singular; but there seems no reason to doubt that the people worshipping the Tope in the Sanchi group are Vajjis, and that these Vajjis, from their dress, &c., are a Northern people, or, in other words, the Yue-chi. If so, we understand how Buddhism was so easily and so heartily received by the Northern tribes of barbarians. Kanishka was one of the Yue-chi; and he invaded Magadha and carried off Asvaghosha, the Buddhist patriarch, to Bactria.[1] This alone would prove that the Yue-chi were already acquainted with Buddhism. Kanishka lived about A.D. 70. We may suppose, therefore, that the Vajjis of Vesâli had exerted an influence among their Northern brethren, at an early period, favourable to the Buddhist faith; and when Kanishka and his tribe openly professed the faith, it was but the consequence of influences that had long been working. It would almost appear as if the name Kapisa (Cabul) were but another for Kapila. Anyhow, the early legends of Buddha's previous history seem to have been carried away to Cabul, as if he had lived there. This, again, seems to favour the Turanian origin of the Sâkyas as a race. Their own legendary history relates that they were first settled at Potala on the Indus, as if they had come down from the mountain region and had settled near the river mouth, whence they spread over the northern portion of India proper. This, combined with other indirect evidence, gives favour to the idea that Buddhism was not a purely indigenous religion of India, but derived from a fusion of Turanian and Aryan elements, and brought out in the teaching of one who was himself perhaps of mixed Aryan and Turanian origin. At

[1] Edkins' Chinese Buddhism, p. 75.

least—and this is what concerns the present inquiry—we can now understand how the religion of Buddha spread so rapidly among the Northern tribes outside of India, and reached at an early period the ears of the Chinese monarch who introduced the first knowledge of this doctrine into his dominions.

2. In my second lecture, I call attention to the fact that the books brought to China from India by the early Buddhist missionaries were written in various Indian dialects, and represent the Buddhism of the districts from which they were brought. It seems to me simply an error to suppose that the Buddhism of India after Aśoka's time was the religion of Magadha only. Doubtless the books belonging to the Southern school, which are written in Pâli, represent the purer faith of the Theravadî school of Buddhists; but that is all. The heretics of Vesâli were probably of non-Indian extraction, and they perverted much of pure Buddhism in their own way. And from them this form of mediæval Buddhism spread northwards and eastwards. The books brought to China were very many of them brought from this Vajjian centre (Léon Féer, "Sûtra of Forty-two Articles"); others were from Cabul, or Kophene, and Gandhâra. Now these were books not written in Pâli, not of the Theravadî school, but of a mixed kind, and probably of a perverted kind, but yet representing the Buddhism of that part of India whence they came. To take an instance: it is well known that in the Pâli canon there is a remarkable book called Dhammapada. This book was evidently of great authority in the Buddhist Church. For that reason it was sought after and translated into various Prakrit dialects. Hence in China we have three if not four distinct works all called "Dhammapada."[1] I say distinct works, because they differ so widely as to make them so. But they are all derived from one common parent, or prototype (as Mr. Rhys Davids says); one of them, the *Fă-kheu-king*, is, I believe, a good translation of the Pâli book known to us through several English versions of it. The *Fa-kheu-pi-u*, which I have trans-

[1] Represented in Chinese by the phonetic symbols *tan-po*; either *Dhammapada* or *Dharmapada*.

lated, is a less faithful copy of the old work, and is accompanied by tales or avadānas, of a grotesque but characteristic form.[1] But there are also two other books in China bearing this same title of Dharmapada (rendered, as I have said, in Chinese by the symbols *Tan-po*, explained by the symbols *Fă-kheu*). These books appear to differ as widely as the last, if not more so, from the Pâli book; but yet they were all translated from Indian originals, at various times, and by various priests; showing us as plainly as possible that there were in India many books bearing titles the same as those found in the South, but not agreeing with those books further than a common tradition would lead us to expect. This is what I have stated in these lectures. But yet there are translations made directly, as it would seem, from Pâli, in China. I have found several of these. The Pari-nibbâna, the Brahmajala, the Sigālovāda, the Dhamma chakka, the Kasībhâradvája, the Mahámangala Suttas; all these I have found and compared with translations from the Pâli, and find that in the main they are identical. I do not say literally the same; they differ in minor points, but are identical in plot and all important details. And when the Vinaya and Âgama collections are thoroughly examined, I can have little doubt we shall find most if not all the Pâli Suttas in a Chinese form.

3. In my third lecture I have called attention to the history and writings of Asvaghosha, the twelfth Buddhist patriarch (according to the Northern school). To this eminent scholar and poet the great change in Buddhist teaching known as the doctrine of the Great Vehicle is mainly due. The point in this development of a vital character is the belief in a force (spiritual force) called Bodhi, existing as the basis of all phenomena. The "heart of Bodhi" is now used to describe a converted or transformed mind. All the converted are

[1] One of these tales, as I have recently discovered from another source (from a work, viz., called *King-liu-seung*), is the story of Rahūla when reproved for falsehood, as found in the book of Avadānas (a canonical work). This tale is referred to in one of the Aśoka Edicts.

Bodhisattvas. They are "sons." Altogether, having translated the Buddhacharita throughout, and also the greater portion of Asvaghosha's sermons, I am impressed with the conviction that Christian teaching had reached his ears at the time when Asvaghosha was in Parthia, or at any rate in Bactria (viz., about A.D. 70), and that he was influenced by it so far as to introduce into Buddhism the changes we find beginning to take shape at this period. The doctrine of a universal salvation, and of Buddha's incarnation by the descent of the Spirit, and of a power of Bodhi or wisdom by which we are made "sons," or converted disciples—these and other non-Buddhist ideas found in Asvaghosha's writings convince me that there was such an intercommunication at this time between East and West as shaped the later school of Buddhism into a pseudo-Christian form; and this accounts very much for some otherwise inexplicable similarities.

It will be evident from this and the next lecture that I cannot believe that Buddhism (I mean as we find it in the Indian writers of the period of Asvaghosha and Deva Bodhisattva) was matured in the valley of the Ganges, or was independent of other movements occurring on the shores of the Mediterranean.

4. In my last lecture I have directed notice to the character of the early myths found in Buddhism as to the cosmic arrangement of the universe. I have no doubt—I can have none—that the idea of a central mountain, and of the rivers flowing from it, and the abode of the gods on its summit—that this is a primitive myth derived from the earliest traditions of our race. I have risked the opinion that "Sumĕ" or "S'um" is a primitive and probably an interjectional sound to represent "the highest," and afterwards was attached to the idea of a high mountain; at least we have "săm" in Chinese for "the heart," which is explained as the "atman," or "highest self," and the symbol representing this is the crescent of the moon and the three "yods" or "dots" above it denoting the highest region of the stars. This is identical with the Chandra vindu of Sanscrit; and the nasal *'m* sound of the latter is simply that of the Chinese "s'ăm" deprived of the invocative

sibilant.[1] But whether this is so or not, I cannot doubt that the Buddhist myth about Sume or Sumeru is distinct from the later Brahmanical account of it, and allied with the universal belief in and adoration of "the highest." I have also traced in the cosmic theory of the Buddhists the early Homeric account of the gods of Olympus. It is singular that we have in the successive stages of the Buddhist Sumeru names so familiar to us as the strong-hoofed (bull), *i.e.*, the sun, the ever-free (Dionysus, or Liber), the chaplet-holders (identified with Taradeva, the stars), the large-eyed (Juno, the full moon), the greatly celebrated (Hephæstus), the earthholder (Poseidon), the extremely fertile (Earth, *ἀρούρα*), and above all the strong *Sakra* (*Ζεύς κράτιστος*). I say it is curious to find this agreement; it can hardly be questioned that the Buddhist cosmic arrangement is allied with Greek tradition, as embodied in Homer.

But I hasten to observe, lastly, that the later Buddhist literature seems to have been affected by intercourse with Syria, and perhaps Samaria. I suppose it cannot be doubted that the intercourse between the Greek Bactrian kingdom and the people of Syria was of a close character. And it is also tolerably certain that there was an early Greek settlement near Samaria. Justin the Martyr belonged to a Greek family settled there, and his allusion to certain *ἀπομνημονεύματα τῶν ἀποστόλων* would indicate that there was a sacred college there of some sort, in which traditions and sayings of holy men were treasured. I have ventured to think that there were Essenes located there, and that many of these were Hellenists. But the rules of the Essene community are almost identical with those of the Buddhists. The agreement is too close to be accidental. Were the Essenes, then, a congregation of lay people corresponding with the Buddhist Upāsakas? The Upāsakas were under vows of chastity, &c., but not so completely as the Bhikshus. A Bhikshu or full Buddhist monk was forbidden to labour in the field, but the Upāsaka was not; the Bhikshu

[1] The sibilant sound is still used before the names or in the presence of great personages in some parts of Japan, to demand silence and as a call for respect.

again wore yellow robes, the Upāsaka wore white garments; the general name for eminent sages or saints (not Bhikshus) was *isayo* (Fausböll, Sutta Nipāta, p. 48), the plural form of *isi*. Another plural form was *isī*; these two agree with the Greek variants *'Εσσαῖοι* and *'Εσσηνοὶ*. Lastly, the three Buddhist stories I have met with relating to the Matangî or low-caste woman, of whom Ananda requested a drink of water (derived apparently from a perversion of the history of the Samaritan woman),—all these considerations led me to believe that there was an early communication between the Hellenists settled near Samaria and the Parthian Buddhists, and, in fact, that much of the hatred of the Jews to the Samaritans was due to this.

Whether right or wrong, to my mind it is no disparagement to the Gospel narrative to suppose such a connection. I have ventured, therefore, to hold to my opinion, and to accept this as a possible explanation of the difficulties which surround the study of Buddhism when regarded as an isolated movement in the religious history of the world.

PLATES.

THE plates here given are copied from those found in Jin ch'au's "History of Buddhism" (*Fă-kiai-lih-t'u*). They are constructed from details found in works of the highest authority, such as the Âgama Sûtras, the Saddharma smriti upasthâna Sûtra, and others.

The figure of Mount Meru, with its terraced slopes, reminds us of the passage in Berosus quoted by Josephus: *καὶ κατεσκεύασε τὸν καλούμενον κρεμαστὸν παράδεισον,* "because his (*i.e.*, Nabuchodonosor's) wife wished to have her native customs, having been brought up in the parts of Media" (Josephus, Antiq., x. 11, 1). This allusion to a hanging paradise suggests the correspondence between the Greek *κρὲμάννυμι* and the Sanscrit *ava-lamb,* both signifying "hanging" or "hanging down;" and if this latter word (*avalamba*) be the root of Olympus, we have here a connection between Meru, as the paradise, and Olympus, as the abode of the gods.[1]

[1] If I understand the words of Strabo, the idea was to make *overhanging* gardens; this is peculiarly Buddhistic.

ADDITIONAL NOTES.

1. The connection between the Homeric system of the gods of Olympus and the Buddhist mythology was first suggested by the evident agreement of the Horæ, as the guardians of the gates of heaven, with the four heavenly kings or *Lokapālitas.* The latter are described in Chinese Buddhist books as originally representing the four seasons, and are the fathers each one of ninety sons, *i.e.*, the ninety days of the quarter. Here the identity is manifest.

2. The fact of there having been a colony of Scyths or Cuthites around Samaria is plainly proved by the allusion of Polybius (Hist., v. 70). The Talmudist writers always speak of the Samaritans as Cutheans, and it is a question whether Simon Magus, in representing himself to be ὁ πρώτος Θέος (Just. Martyr, Apolog., i.),[1] and also "the great power of God" and "some great one," was not merely using well-recognised Buddhist terms, viz. (1.) Adi Buddha (known as the *first* Buddha as early as the beginning of our era, under the form in Chinese of *Yih-sin*); (2.) Dasabāla Buddha; and (3.) Mahesi. His death, too, occurring from a fall when attempting to fly, is peculiarly applicable to his imposture as a Buddhist Rishi or *isi.*

[1] S. Justini Martyris cum Tryphone Dialogus, p. 351, n.—Ed. Samuel Jebb. 1729.

CORRECTIONS AND ADDITIONS.

Page 3, *note* 1. *Chu-fă-lan* is restored to Gobhinanda, or Gobananda, by the Thibetans.

Page 5, *line* 8. *For* "*King-kwong*" *read* "*Kin-kwang.*"

Page 8, *line* 29. When I say "a translation of Dhammapada," I cannot be supposed to imply that it is translated from the Pāli copy of that work, but simply that the symbols *Fă-kheu* are themselves said to be a translation of *Tan-po*, *i.e.*, Dhammapada, or Dharmapada.

Page 20, *line* 13. Dharmâkshaya may also be restored to Dharmâkshara, or Dharmaraksha.

Page 31, *line* 25. *For* "Śâkra" *read* "Śakra," and in all subsequent cases.

Page 95, *line* 2. *For* "Asvaghosha" *read* "Aśvaghosha," and in all subsequent cases.

[For many mistakes in accents the author requests his readers' indulgence.]

that Buddhist books were known in China before the time of She Hwang-ti (B.C. 221). This monarch, as is well known, claimed to be the first universal emperor. This claim he put forth in the twenty-sixth year of his reign as Chêng Wang. He built the Great Wall and destroyed all the books; and Fa-lin con-

[1] The Buddhist Tripiṭaka, as it is known in China and Japan. A Catalogue and Compendious Report. By Samuel Beal, 1876.

FOUR LECTURES.

LECTURE I.

EARLY TRANSLATORS OF BUDDHIST BOOKS IN CHINA.

THE object of these Lectures will be to bring before you some notices respecting Buddhism and Buddhist books in China and Japan.

The phrase "Chinese Buddhism," as it is sometimes used, is misleading. We might as well speak of "Chinese Christianity." Buddhism and Buddhist books in China are the same as they were in India; and, with respect to the latter at least, the same as they now are in Ceylon. For I can have no doubt that the books belonging to the Buddhist Canon, as it is known in that country, will be found, with few exceptions, to exist in China; and to this I shall call your attention hereafter. The mere circumstance of these books being translated into Chinese cannot alter their character, any more than the translation of our own Sacred Books from the Greek or Hebrew can alter *theirs*.

It is still a question when Buddhism was introduced into China. There is a work (*Po-tse-lun*, Catalogue,[1] Case lxxxvii. p. 95), written by one Fa-lin, to confute the sceptical opinions of Fu-yi, in which the writer brings a mass of evidence to show that Buddhist books were known in China before the time of She Hwang-ti (B.C. 221). This monarch, as is well known, claimed to be the first universal emperor. This claim he put forth in the twenty-sixth year of his reign as Chêng Wang. He built the Great Wall and destroyed all the books; and Fa-lin con-

[1] The Buddhist Tripiṭaka, as it is known in China and Japan. A Catalogue and Compendious Report. By Samuel Beal, 1876.

tends that among these were the Buddhist Scriptures (k. i. p. 10). He also records the anecdote (which appears also in the great Encyclopædia of Kang-hsi, *sub* "Shih-kia") that in the time of She Hwang there was a foreign Buddhist priest, Li Fang, who, with seventeen companions, came to China with Buddhist books for the purpose of converting the king. The emperor, however, shut them up in prison. In the evening six men (of superhuman character) came and with their diamond maces opened the prison doors and brought the captives out. On this the emperor was filled with fear and worshipped them.

This fable need not be accepted. Fa-lin contends that both Confucius and Laou Tseu spoke of Buddha; he says that once Confucius was asked if he was a Holy man (shing), to which the sage replied that he was not. What, then, are the three kings (wang) Holy men? To which he replied they were wise men, but not holy. What, then, are the five kings (ti) Holy men? To which he replied they were virtuous and truthful, but not holy. What, then, were the three emperors (hwang) Holy men? To which he replied they were prudent, but not holy. And when he was asked, Who, then, is the Holy man? then Fu-sze, greatly moved, said, "The western region has a Holy man—without striving he is self-governed (without confusion); he speaks not, and yet is the truth (or, sincere); he teaches not, and yet his own conduct how deep! how deep!"

Then, with respect to Laou Tseu, he quotes various writers to show that he was identical with Buddha. One says, "The Master, transforming himself, went to India, and entered Nirvāna;" another says, "The Master of the Laou people (*i.e.*, the Taouists) was Śâkya Muni."

Again, he contends that the falling rocks and stars in the reign of Chwang Wang, of the Chow dynasty, were the portents that occurred at Buddha's birth.

But all these notices and contentions may be dismissed as more or less fabulous, and we may be content to place the introduction of Buddhism into China about the time of the first diffusion of the Christian doctrine in the West. Whether there be any connection between these two events is, I still think, an open question; one thing, at least, we know, that it was just at the time when Buddhism was brought to China that the dispersion of Jews and Christians occurred consequent on the troubles in Judæa. Du Halde and the old writers may not be wrong, then, in supposing that some knowledge of great events, other than the teaching of Buddha, had reached China at this time, and led to the mission to India about which I now proceed to speak.

The Vision of Ming Ti.

During the after-Han dynasty of the family Liu, which reigned at Loyang (the eastern capital), there appeared to Ming Ti, the second emperor, in the third year of the Yung P'ing period (*i.e.*, A.D. 60) [the cyclical characters being *Kang Shin*], in a dream, a golden flying figure, above his head the glory of the sun and moon, which hovered above the vestibule of the palace. On inquiry, the historiographer, Fu-yih, said he had heard that there was a Divine Being (*Shin*) in the West, called Buddha, who had come down to earth, and that the dream had something to do with this. Accordingly, A.D. 64 [*Shin tseu*], the emperor selected from his officers Ts'ai Yin, Ts'in King (the rank *Poh sse*), Wang Tsun, and others, all numbering eighteen men, to go to the West to inquire about the religion of Buddha.

Yin and the rest coming to the country of India invited Kasyapa Matanga and Dharmananda[1] to return with them, who, using a white horse for carriage, came back with books, pictures, and an image of Sâkya Buddha, A.D. 67, to Loyang. The emperor rejoiced at the event, erected a temple, called the White Horse Temple, which was finished on the first month of the fourteenth year of his reign, A.D. 71. On this occasion the Taouist priests of the Five Mountains,[2] Shen Sin and others, being dissatisfied, sent a deputation to the emperor exhorting him to have their respective merits tried. On which occasion the emperor, having called an assembly before the southern gate of the White Horse Temple, the Taouist priests put their sacred books and religious paraphernalia (spiritual treasures) on the eastern altar; the

[1] So I restore *Chu-fă-lan*. The prefix *Chu* (Indian) is not a component part of his name.

[2] Five high peaks, worshipped in China, viz., *Tung-yoh*, in Shantung; *Sai-yoh*, in Shensi, south of the capital; *Nan yoh*, in Hunan, near the centre; *Pih yoh*, in the south-west of Chihili; *Chung yoh*, in the west of Honan, near the Yellow River.

emperor placed the sacred books, relics, and images of Buddha above the hall of the seven gems, on the west.

And now the Taouist priests, with tears, called on the Heavenly Lord, whilst they lay prostrate on the ground; then, placing sandal-wood on the altar and burning their books, they hoped, as in former times, that others would arise from the ashes and ascend into the air and exhibit wonderful changes. But no such event now occurred, nor could they recite their sacred incantations as they ought. On this the great officer, Chang Yen, addressing them, said, "Your trial has failed; your pretensions are false; the religion of the western countries is the true religion."

Then the priests of the Nan yoh, Shuh tsai and others, self-convicted, fell dead. After this the *sariras* of Buddha, emitting the five colours, ascending into the air, formed themselves, as it were, into a covering over the assembly, glorious as the disc of the sun. Matanga, the Doctor of the Law, having before this arrived at the condition of a Rahat, forthwith, by his miraculous power, ascended up into space and there exhibited himself, undergoing various spiritual changes, *e.g.*, flying, walking, sitting, sleeping, and so on.

Hereupon there was a rain of precious flowers, so that the feelings of the beholders were deeply moved, and they rejoiced exceedingly. On this, whilst Matanga was seated (in the air), Dharmananda preached a sermon, and multitudes of the people were converted. Amongst these, the royal ladies, the emperor's chief housekeeper (*tsich u*), and others, 190 persons, all became professed disciples (*ch'uh kia*); of the great officers of state, civil and military, 268 became disciples; of the Taouists belonging to the "four peaks," Lu-hwui-tung and others, 620 men became disciples; of the capital town, 391 of the chief men and women became disciples. Of the royal family, those who had professed religion, with their heads shaved, offered gifts and presents to the Sacred Books for thirty days, after which they founded temples—seven outside the city, three within. In the seven the priests located themselves, in the three the female disciples dwelt. All this is related in the annals of the Han dynasty under the heading, "*Ming Ti pen niu chouen.*"

NAMES OF TRANSLATORS.

The Shaman Kia-yeh-mo-teng (Kasyapa Matanga).

He was a man of Middle India, of the Brahman caste. When young he was distinguished for talent; with ardent purpose he studied various treatises, and extracted from them new and hidden meanings. Moved by the Divine Spirit, he went into Western India, where he was invited by a small country to come over and explain the *King-Kwong-Ming-King* (Suvarṇa prabhâsa Sûtra) to them. Just at this time a neighbouring state attempted to march an army into the former country, but they were unable to advance over the frontiers. Suspecting some secret agency, they sent messengers to find out (by augury) the reason of the hindrance. Having entered the country they found the king with his ministers, &c., quietly listening to the Sûtra of the Great Development, whilst a divine spirit was protecting the country. On this they were converted, and it was just then that T'sai yin and the other emissaries from China met Matanga, and brought him to Loyang to the emperor, A.D. 67.

This priest, located in the White Horse Temple, translated "The Sûtra of 42 Paragraphs," I vol.

[This Sûtra was copied from other foreign books. Matanga, using his great insight, when he first taught the people, as their faith was little, put together these excellent sections, not giving the people at once full books, but only portions of books, to act as guides to them in their unenlightened condition. Matanga died afterwards in Loyang.—*Ch. Ed.*]

The Shaman Chu-fă-lan (Dharmananda).

This priest was also of Middle India. At an early age he exhibited great talent and fondness for Buddhist books, especially the Vinaya. He could recite more than a hundred myriad words from the Sûtras. Although hospitality was freely offered him, he was not content to remain at home, but desired to travel to make known the true doctrine. Contrary to the wish of the ruler of the country, he secretly left with Matanga, and after travelling with him came to China, where during Kung Ti's reign he assisted in the translation of the "Sutra of 42 Paragraphs." After Matanga's death Nanda, from the year A.D. 68 to A.D. 70, translated alone other Sûtras.

Of these the following is a list:—

1. Fŏ-pen-hing-king, ... 5 kiouen.
2. Shih-ti-twan-kie-king, . . . 4 „
3. Fă-hai-tsong-king, ... 3 „
4. Fŏ-pen-sing-king, ... 2 „
5. 'Rh-pih-luh-shih-kiai-hoh-i, . . 2 „

Altogether 5 distinct works in 16 chapters. Of these No. 1 is the earliest translation known of the "Life of Buddha"—it is now lost. No. 4 is a book of Jâtakas also lost.

It is recorded of this priest that when the emperor Wu Ti (140 B.C.) had cleaned out (bored through) the Kwan-Ming lake and had discovered some black ashes among the excavated stuff, he asked Tung-fang So about it, whereupon So said, "You must ask the Tartars (hu-jin) of the Western world." When Nanda arrived, therefore, he was asked about it, and replied, "These are the ashes of the world burnt up in the Kalpa past."

This priest, again, when he came to Loyang, caused a picture to be made from the sandal-wood image of Buddha done by King Udâyana, and reverence to be paid it.

The Shaman Chi-lo-kia-chin (Shirgatchin).

This priest was a Hun (White Hun). Moved by a desire to convert the world (*mat*, "things"), he came to China in the year 147 A.D., and worked at translations till A.D. 187 in Loyang.

In all he completed 21 distinct translations, comprising 63 chapters, of which I will name the following:—

1. A-kieu-Fo-kwo-king,. . . . 2 kiouen
2. Pan-jo-tao-hing-p'hin, . . . 10 „
3. Shen-ling-yan-king, ... 2 „
4. Pao-tsih-king, ... 1 „

Of these, No. 1 is an account of the land of Akshobya—one of the Dhyâni Buddhas. From this we gather that the development of these fanciful Buddhas had already taken a distinct form before the year 147 A.D.

No. 2 is a section from the Prâjna Paramita Sûtra, which shows that this work dates also before this period.

No. 3 is a translation of the Sûtra commonly called Śurangama, though I think it should more properly be restored to Śringin, *i.e.*, "the horned," referring to the highest rays of the sun, which are compared to horns, and so denoting the highest flight of doctrine. This horned figure is symbolised in various ways from the simple circle (of the sun) with its rays, as on the Buddha-Gayá rail (Bhilsa Topes, p. 333), advancing to the common Trisul figure at Sanchi, where, however, instead of the sun we have the Lotus flower. This highest flight of doctrine so symbolised thus became the "*in excelsis*" of the later Buddhists, under the form of "mani-padme."[1] The Sûtra we refer to is in two chapters, the later one, translated in the Tang dynasty by Paramita and Meghasikhi, is in *ten* kiouen. This is accounted for by the usual process of development or expansion. We notice that Fa-hien, when he recited the Sûtra called by this name in the Vulture-Peak Mountain, must have used the shorter one, probably the one under present notice.

No. 4 is the Ratnakûta Sutra, but very short, being in one kiouen.

The Shaman 'An-tsing or Sai-kao.

This missionary was a prince royal of Parthia (*'An-sih;* either of the country of the Arsacidæ, or the Assakas, or *ἱππάσιοι*, *i.e.*, Parthians). When his father died he gave up the kingdom to his uncle and became a Buddhist recluse. He came to China in the second year of the reign of Hwan-ti, the title being *Kien-ho, i.e.*, A.D. 149, and soon distinguished himself by his knowledge of Chinese. He went to Kwangchau (Canton) to encounter an old associate of his who in former days (*i.e.*, in a previous birth) had possessed a fiery and passionate temper. As he went along the road, a young man armed with a knife attacked and wounded him. Kao with a smile addressed him and said, "I have come here to see you." Afterwards with the same object he went again towards Canton; on the way, in the Kung pavilion in Hu-nan, he entered a temple where sailors were

[1] The *gem, i.e.*, the trisul, *in the Lotus;* and so it is everywhere figured.

wont to offer sacrifices and pray, in fear of a monster that dwelt in the river. Kao, fearing that this monster, whose days were now near at an end, would pollute the river when dead, caused him to be transported to a marsh (*tsch chung*) in Shensi. Before this, however, he caused his head to appear, and he spoke to him in the Hu language, on which the monster shed tears. Afterwards, to prevent his birth in hell, Sai-ko devoted 1000 pieces of silk stuff and various gems to the building of a tower (pagoda). After the foundations had been dug and a year or so elapsed, suddenly some prayers (written forms of incantation) disappeared; on which Kao said that the monster had escaped from his unhappy condition. Afterwards in the marsh at Shensi men discovered the head and tail of a large boa (*mong*), in length many *li*; and now in the prefecture of Sin-Yang there is a hamlet called the Snake village (*Shie ts'un*). This is the place.

Afterwards Sai-Kao went to Canton, where he was killed in a popular tumult in the market-place.

From A.D. 149 to A.D. 171 he translated 176 distinct works in 197 chapters. Of these I will name the following:—

1. Fă-kheu-king,	4	kiouen
2. Wou-liang-sheu-king,	2	"
3. Sse-ti-king,	1	"
4. Pa-ching-to-king,	1	"
5. Shih-i-in-ün-king,	1	"
6. Chun-fă-lun-king,	1	"
7. She-kia-lo-yue-king,	1	"
8. Ku-mu-song-yih-tseu,	1	"

No. 1 is a translation of Dhammapada. I have not yet been able to ascertain if this book is lost or not. If not, it would be very interesting to compare it with later editions of the same work.

No. 2. This is a translation of Amitâyus Sûtra, or the Amitâbha Sûtra. Being of so early a date, it is interesting.

No. 3. This is the Sûtra of the "Four Great Truths" (*cattári ariyasaccáni*), on which Buddha founded his system.

No. 4. This is the Sûtra of the "Eight Correct or Orthodox Ways" (*Ariyo aṭṭhaṅgiko maggo*), concerning which so much has been written.

No. 5. This is the Sûtra of the Twelve Nidânas or Connections, by which Buddha in a later period of his teaching tried to account for the origin and destruction of finite existence.

No. 6. This is the Sûtra sometimes called the "Foundation of the Kingdom of Righteousness," otherwise "Turning the Wheel of the Law." It was the first sermon preached by Buddha. He had gone to Benares after his enlightenment, and there by this sermon converted five ascetics who had formerly been his companions. Both this and the former sermon are known in China. They differ in no material respect from the translations from the Pâli of the same sermons (*Pâli Suttas*).[1]

No. 7. This is the Sigālavada Sûtra, which has been translated from Pâli by the late Professor Childers[2] and partly by myself from the Chinese.[3]

No. 8. I quote this merely because of its singular title, "The Widow Woman at the Funeral of her only Son." I do not know whether it is still extant.

The Shaman Chu-fo-so, and others.

(1) *Chu-fo-so*, a Shaman of India who came to China in the Hi P'ing year of the reign of Ling Ti, A.D. 172, and translated until A.D. 184 two works.

(2) *To-wei-'an-yüan*, a Upasaka from Parthia, came to China A.D. 182, and translated at Loyang 2 works.

(3) The Shaman *Chi-yau*, an Indian, came to China A.D. 186, and translated at Loyang 11 works in 13 chapters. Among these is the *Siu-pen-k'i-king* in 2 chapters, a primitive work, being a Life of Buddha. There is another translation also, the Sûtra of Mahâmaya, the mother of Buddha, which would be interesting if discovered.

(4) The Shaman *Hong-shin*, a man of the western world, who travelled about in the work of converting men, and came to China A.D. 188, and translated at Loyang one work, viz., Wen-ti-yuh-sse-king (*Questions Concerning Affairs in Hell*).

(5) A pious layman called *Yan-Fo-Tiau* of *Lin-hwai* trans-

---

[1] By Mr. Rhys Davis, in the *Sacred Books of the East*.

[2] *The Whole Duty of the Buddhist Layman*: Contemporary Review, February 1876.

[3] *Catalogue*, &c., p. 112.

lated, A.D. 189, in conjunction with 'An-yuan, 7 works in 10 chapters.

(6) The Shaman *Kong-mang-tsiang*, a western man, of much erudition, came to China A.D. 194, and translated at Loyang, till A.D. 200, 6 works in 9 chapters, among which I observe a copy of the Brahmajâla Sûtra (*Fan-kong-king*) in 2 chapters, and also a Life of Buddha with the title *Ta-tseu-pen-k'i-sui-ying-king*, in 2 chapters. This last work is still extant, and has been referred to in my Catalogue, &c., p. 116. He also edited another translation of the Sûtra of the "Four Truths."

(7) The Shaman *Ta-lih*, a man of the west, came to China A.D. 199, and translated at Loyang, in conjunction with the last-named priest, a Life of Buddha called Shiu-hing-pen-k'i-king, in 2 chapters. This work is still extant, and has been referred to, *J. R. A. S.*, vol. x., part iii., p. 356.

(8) The Shaman *Tan-kwo* (Dharmaphala), a man of the west, brought to China a copy of a Life of Buddha, which he had procured at Kapilavastu (another account tells us he had got it from a descendant of Buddha's uncle), in the year 208 A.D. The work in question is called *Chung-pen-k'i-king*.[1] It is said to be taken from the Dirghâgama collection; it begins with the first sermon at Benares.

Besides the above, during the Han dynasty there were made translations of 123 works in 148 chapters, the names of the translators being lost.

[The names of these works are given in the *Ku-kin-tsi-king-t'u-ki.*]

During the Wei Dynasty of the Family of Ts'au, A.D. 220–260.

(1) The Shaman Dharmakala (*Tan-ko-kia-lo*), an Indian. When young he devoted himself to study; he could recite throughout the four Vedas, and was well acquainted with the five Vidya Shasters. Having become a Buddhist, he diligently studied the works of the Great and Little Vehicle and the different copies of the Vinaya. He came to China in the year

[1] It is to be found in the volume of Sûtras, *Miscellaneous*, Case 32.

223 A.D., where he flourished till A.D. 251. He laboured, translating principally works belonging to the Vinaya, at Loyang, among which I observe *Săng-chi-kiai-pen*, that is, the original rules of the Mahāsañghika school, in one chapter. This was the first book on the Vinaya rules translated in China.

(2) The Shaman *Kong-sang-k'ai*, a man of India, of great erudition and a deep searcher into the abstruse meaning of the Sûtras, came to China A.D. 253, and resided in the White Horse Temple of Loyang; translated 2 works, the second of which is another version of the *Wou-liang-sheu-king, i.e.*, the Sûtra of Boundless Years.

(3) The Shaman *Tan-ti*, a Parthian, well versed in the Vinaya literature, translated at Loyang in the year 254 A.D. the Kamma rules according to the Dharmagupta school (*Tañ-wou-ti-kie-mi*) in 2 chapters.

(4) The Shaman *Pih-yen*, a man of the western countries, very shrewd in the interpretation of the Yoga Shasters, came to China A.D. 259, and translated whilst dwelling in the White Horse Temple at Loyang six works in eight chapters, among which I notice a second version of the Śurangama (Śringin) Sûtra in two chapters.

(5) The Shaman *'An-fă-hien*, who, after travelling through various countries, came to China (date not given, but it must have been before A.D. 260), and translated *Lo-mo-kia-king* in 3 chapters. This appears to be a history of Rāma. Also, *Ta-pan-ni-pwan-king*, in 2 chapters. This is the Mahaparinirvâna Sutra.

During the Wu Dynasty of the Family of Sün,
A.D. 222–264.

(1) The Upasaka *Chi-hien*, his private name being *Kung Ming*, a Hun (White Hun), came to China towards the end of the Han dynasty, was remarkable for his thin lanky body and his yellowish eyes. In the second year of the period *Hwang-wu* (A.D. 224), till the second year of *Kien-hing* (A.D. 254), he laboured at translations, producing 129 distinct works in 152 chapters. Among these I observe another version of the

Mahaparinirvāna Sûtra in 2 chapters, also another copy of the *Sui-ying-pen-k'i-king* in 2 chapters; the *O-mi-to* (Amitābha) Sûtra, in 2 chapters; the expanded (*fang-tang*) Śurangama Sûtra, 2 chapters; the *Fa-kheu* (Dhammapada) in 2 chapters; the *Lung-shi-niu-king* in 1 chapter (this is probably the history of Elapatra); and latterly another version of the Sûtra of 42 Paragraphs, with several copies of the Âgama Sûtras (the Nikâyas of the South).

(2) The Shaman *Wei-chi-lan*, an Indian, well versed in the Sûtras and Âgamas, travelled about teaching; he came with another Shaman, *Chu-liu-yen*, from the western countries to *Wu-chang* (the capital of the Wu dynasty) in 225 A.D., and there translated the two works—

1. *A-cha-mo-king*, the Âgama Sûtra, in 4 chapters.

2. *Fa-kheu-tsih-king* (Dhammapada), 2 chapters.

(3) The Shaman *Chu-liu-yen*, a fellow-traveller of the last, came to China in the year 231 A.D., and translated 3 works in 4 chapters.

(4) The Shaman *Kong-sang-ui*, a man of Samarcand, and the eldest son of the principal chief of the country, was taken to India at an early age, and having lost both his parents, he became a recluse. Coming to China in the year 242 A.D., he laboured in founding Pagodas till 248 A.D. He then procured some She-li (śarîras, *relics*), brilliant as the heavens and of five colours, which the king being unable to destroy, he erected over them a Śarîra pagoda, and founded a Buddhist temple. In A.D. 253 he translated 10 works in 29 chapters, among which I observe:—

1. *Taou-shü-king*, the Sûtra of the Tree of Knowledge (Bodhidruma), with explanations.

2. *King-min-wang-king*, the Sûtra of the Bright-faced King, which I take to be the same as Śibirâja (Śivirâja).

(5) The Shaman *Chi-k'iang*, a man of the west, came to China in the second year of the period Wu-fêng, A.D. 256, and there he translated the following work in 6 chapters:—*Fă-hwa-san-mui-king* (Pundarika Samâdhi Sûtra).

Besides the above, there were 110 works in 291 chapters translated during this dynasty, the names of the translators being lost.

Among these I observe—

1. *Ts'a-pi-u-king*, the Sûtra of Mixed Comparisons (miscellaneous tales).

2. *Mo-ho-shing-king* (Mahâyana Sûtra), in 14 chapters.

3. *Mo-ho-yen-yau-po-ti-she-king*, the Mahâyana Upadeśa Sûtra, 5 chapters.

4. *San-mui-wang-king*, the Samâdhi Râja Sûtra, in 5 chapters.

5. *Shi-ti-hwan-in-sho-wen*, the Questions of Śakradevendra, in 3 chapters.

The Western Tsin Dynasty, A.D. 265–313.

(1) The Shaman Dharmaraksha, a Hun, became a disciple at eight years of age, came to China A.D. 265, and worked at translation till 313 A.D. He produced altogether 210 volumes in 394 chapters. Among these I observe versions of the *Wou-liang-sheu-king* (the Sûtra of Boundless Years), in 2 chapters; of the Śurangama Sûtra, in 2 chapters; and of the Mahâparinirvâna Sûtra, in 2 chapters.

(2) The Shaman *Kiang-liang-lu-chi* (Kâlaruchi, although the Chinese interpretation is said to be "*true* joy"), a man of the west, came to China A.D. 281, and residing in Canton, translated one Sûtra in 1 chapter.

(3) The Shaman *'An-fă-kin*, a Parthian, a man of large reading, came to China about A.D. 302, and worked at translation till A.D. 306 in Loyang. He produced 5 books in 12 chapters.

(4) The Shaman *Wou-lo-yau-ché*, a man of Khoten, came to China A.D. 293, and translated the Light-giving Prajña Sûtra in 20 chapters.

[It appears that *Wou-lo* had lost his original copy of this Sûtra, on which he sent his disciple, *Fo-u-tan*, back to Khoten to get another. But on the way, before he arrived at Khoten, he gave up his faith and denounced the book before the king as contrary to Buddha's teaching. On this they tried to burn it, but it refused to be destroyed, and only emitted a bright and wonderful light; on which the king and his ministers were impressed with religious fear, and attributed the miracle to divine interposition.]

(5) The Shaman *Chu-shuh-lan*, a man of the-west, had, on a

former occasion, in the reign of Hwei-Ti, of the Western Tsin dynasty, travelled as far as China on his work of conversion. He translated in Loyang 2 volumes, 3 kiouen.

Among these is a copy of the Śurangama Sûtra (Śringin) in 2 kiouen.

(6) The Shaman *Pih-fă-tsu*, of *Kong-niu* ("Within the River"). His secular name was *Wan-shi.* He became a disciple at an early age. He was devoted to the study of the Sacred Books, and each day would recite from eight to nine thousand words. He thoroughly investigated the Vaipulya books, and built a Vihâra at Chang'an. He was well versed in Sanscrit (Fan) and the Tsin language (Chinese), and in the reign of Hwei-ti translated 23 books in 25 chapters.

Among these I observe—

1. The Nirvâna Sûtra, in 2 chapters. [From its brevity, this would probably be the Southern copy.]

2. The Parinirvāna of Mahâ Prajāpati. [*Ta-ngai-tao-pan-ni-pan-king.*]

(7) The Shaman *Chi-fă-to* translated in the *Yung-ning* year of Hwei-ti (301 A.D.) 4 works in 5 kiouen.

(8) The Upasaka *Shih-tao-chi* translated in the *Ta-k'ang* (for *Yung-k'ang*) year of Wu-ti (A.D. 300), to the end of the *Yung-kia* year (312 A.D.) of Hwai-ti, some Sûtras copied by Fa-hu (Dharmaraksha), but which he had left untranslated at his death. In all he thus translated 54 volumes in 66 chapters.

Among these I observe the following:—

Kwan-shi-yin-shau-ki-king, i.e., the Previous History of Kwan-yin, in 1 chapter.

[The remainder relate principally to different Bodhisatwas.]

(9) The Shaman *Fă-lih*, in the reign of Hwei-ti (290–300 A.D.), dwelt at Loyang with the Shaman *Fă-ku*, and there translated 4 books in 13 chapters. Among these I notice—

1. The *Lau-tan-king*, in 6 vols. This is the Pindadána Sûtra.[1]

2. *Fă-k'eu-pen-mi-king* (Beginnings and Endings of Dhammapada).

After Fă-lih's death, *Fă-ku* translated alone 132 volumes in

[1] Referred to in my *Catalogue*, p. 39.

142 chapters. Among these I notice another copy of the Piṇḍadána Sûtra, in 8 chapters.

3. The History of the Female Demon (Mo), who, after hearing Buddha preach, obtained a man's body. [1 chapter.] [*Mo-niu-wen-Fo-shwo-fă-teh-nan-shin.*]

4. The Story of the Marriage of Yu-ye, the Son of Videhî. [*Wei-ti-hi-tseu-Yue-yé-wen-fu-yin-king.*]

5. The History of the Death of King Prasenajit's Mother. [*Po-sse-nih-wang-song-mu-king.*]

6. The Parinirvāna of Suddhodana Râja (*Tsing-fan-wang-pan-ni-pan-king*).

7. The Prophecy of Ajasat's Final Release. [*A-che-si-wang-shau-kiuh-king.*]

In the Catalogue of the Tripiṭaka published during the above dynasty (the Western Tsin), 8 other works are named, published during the reign of Hwei-ti, in the Yuän K'ang year (291 A.D.)

Besides the above, there are 8 books in 15 chapters, the names of the translators being lost.

The Eastern Tsin, of the Sze Ma Family.

[Capital, Kien K'ang.]

(1) The Shaman *Pi-si-li-mih-to-lo, i.e.*, the Fortunate Friend (Śrimitra), a man of the western countries, and the eldest son of a râja, came in his travels to Kien K'ang and there founded the Kien-cho Temple (*i.e.*, the first temple of Kien). He was commonly called the *Kao-tso-fă-sse* (the High-throned Doctor). He translated (A.D. 322) 3 books in 11 chapters. Among these were:—

1. The Sûtra of Anointing a King (Abhishekha), in nine chapters.

2. The Dhârani of the Great Peacock King.

3. Mixed Dhârani of the Great Peacock King.

(2) The Shaman *Che-to-lin* having set out on his travels for the benefit of the world, came to China, and in the first year of Chêng-ti (326 A.D.) translated 2 works, viz.:—

1. The Lotus of the Good Law Expanded (*Fang-teng-fă-hwa-king*), 5 chapters.

2. The section relating to the conversion of the Bodhisatwas

belonging to the land of Akshobya (*A-chu-fo-t'sa-chu-pu-sa-hioh-chêng-phin*), in 2 chapters.

(3) The Shaman *Chu-tan-wou-lan*, *i.e.*, Integrity of the Law (Dharmananda), [observe that *chu* in this and other cases is an honorific expletive], a man of the western world, came to China (A.D. 382), and worked at translation till the twentieth year of the period *T'ai Yuän* (A.D. 396), and translated altogether 111 books in 120 chapters. Among these are—

1. Agreements and Differences as to the 260 Rules of the Three Schools, two chapters [*i.e.*, of the Pratimoksha in the different schools].

2. The Names of the one Thousand Buddhas of the Bhadra Kalpa.

3. The Sûtra of Yuh-ye.

4. Aśoka cherishes the Bodhi Tree [referring to the destruction and revival of the tree].

(4) The Shaman *Kiu-tan-säng-kia-ti-po*, *i.e.*, Gotamasañgha Deva, a man of Cophene, came to China and translated altogether 50 chapters (A.D. 344). Afterwards, in the year 392 A.D., he translated 3 other works in 7 chapters, and again 2 other works in 31 chapters. Altogether he translated 8 distinct works in 167 chapters.

Among these were several works of the Abhidharma class, as—

1. The Abhidarma Hṛidaya.

2. The Vibhasha Abhidharma.

And again—

3. The Middle Âgama Sûtra.

4. The Add-one Âgama Sûtra.

(5) The Shaman *Kia-lau-to-kia*, that is, Kaludaka, a man of the west, who came to China A.D. 390, and translated 1 book in 1 chapter.

(6) The Shaman *K'ang Tao* came to China A.D. 394, and translated one work in 3 chapters.

(7) The Shaman *Fo-to-p'o-to-lo*, *i.e.*, Buddhabhadra, whose private name was Sâkya, a man of Kapilavastu, and a descendant of Amritodana Râja [the uncle of Sâkya Muni]. He became a disciple at five years of age, and daily read a thousand words of the Scriptures. His fellow-student, Sañghadatta, while lost in

meditation, once saw Bhadra appear suddenly, and asking him whence he came, he said he had been to the Tusita heaven to see Maitreya. [Other remarkable events are recorded of him, especially relating to his voyage with a priest, *Che-yan.*] He met Kumārajiva in China, and from A.D. 399 to A.D. 422 he worked at translation, partly in the capital, and partly in Mount Lu. Altogether, he translated 15 books in 125 chapters, among which I observe—

1. *Kwo-hu-in-kwo-king.* A valuable Life of Buddha in 4 chapters.

2. A new Amitâyus Sûtra, in 2 chapters.

3. The Vinaya of the Sañgha (Mahâsañgha) school, in 30 chapters.

(8) The Shaman *Tan-ma-pi* (Virtue of the Law) came to China A.D. 406, and, in compliance with the request of twenty priests, translated the *Tsa-wen-lui-sz* in 2 chapters.

(9) The Shaman *Pi-mo-lo-ch'a* (Vimalâksha), a man of Cophene (Cabul), remarkable for his blue eyes, and so called the blue-eyed Doctor, dwelt formerly in *Kiu-sse* (Karashar), crossed the sandy deserts with Kumārajiva, and arrived in China in the eighth year of the Hung-she period, 408 A.D. After the latter's death in the year 412 A.D., he translated many works belonging to the Vinaya, especially the *Shih-song-liu, i.e.*, the Vinaya of the Sarvâstavâdins.

(10) The Shaman *Fă-hien,* his family name Kung, a man of Wu-Yang, in the prefecture of Ping Yang, he became a disciple at three years of age. Being desirous to obtain religious books, especially the Vinaya, he vowed to go abroad to seek them, and so in the third year of the period Lung-ngan of the reign of Ngan-ti (A.D. 400) [there is some little difficulty here, as Mayers gives the cyclic year 399 A.D.] he set out for India. He worshipped the sacred traces and learned the Fan language, and acquired a facility in writing that language with the greatest exactness. In A.D. 405 he set out on his return, and translated in the capital, in the Tao-Yang Temple, 5 works in 23 chapters. Among these are the—

1. Mahâparinirvāna Sûtra, in 5 chapters.
2. The Expanded Parinirvāna Sûtra, in 2 chapters.

(11) The Shaman *Chi-ma-to,* a western man, travelling so far

as the Tsin country (China), translated 25 books in 46 chapters. One of these I observe to be the *Samantamukha* section of the Saddharma Pundarika Sûtra.

(12) The Householder called Nanda, a man of the west, came to China A.D. 319, and translated 2 works in 4 chapters.

(13) The Shaman *Chu-fă-lih*, a man of the west, came to China A.D. 319, and translated 1 work in 1 chapter.

(14) The Shaman *Kao-kung* translated 4 works in 6 chapters.

(15) The Shaman *Shih-lang-kung* translated 1 work.

(16) The Shaman *Shih-fă-yung* translated 1 book.

Other books, the names of translators lost, 52 in number in 56 chapters.

(17) The Shaman *Tan-mo-chi* (Sea of the Law) came to China A.D. 431, and with Fă-nien in Chang'an translated 2 works in 2 chapters, one of which is the "Rules of the Bhikshunis according to the Sarvâstavâdins."

(18) The Shaman *Shih-hwei-shang* laboured with the former and Fă-nien, and in the year A.D. 432 translated the great Rules of the Bhikshunis, 1 chapter.

(19) The Shaman *Kiu-mo-lo-fo-te* (Kumârabodhi), a western man, laboured with Fo-hu and others in the work of translation down to the year 435 A.D. in Chang'an; he produced 1 work.

(20) The Shaman *Săng-kia-po-ch'ing* (Seen of All, or Universally Seen), a Cophene (Cabul) man, translated, A.D. 445, in conjunction with *Shah-tao-ngan* and others, the Abhidharma Vibasha Shastra, 1 book, 14 chapters, and also the works of Vasumitra and of Sañgha-raksha; altogether 3 books in 17 chapters.

(21) The Shaman *Tan-mo-ping* (Love of the Law), an Indian, translated with *Chu-fo-nien*, A.D. 446, in Chang'an, and produced a copy of the Mahaprajñaparamita Sûtra from a MS., 1 book, 5 chapters.

(22) The Shaman Dharmananda, a Turk (Turkhâra), travelled through many countries, and at last came to China A.D. 448, and translated 5 works in 116 chapters, among which are—

1. The Middle Âgama, in 59 chapters.
2. The Mixed Âgama, in 51 chapters.

The Yaou Thsin Period. [Capital, Chang'an.]

(1) The Shaman *Chu-fo-nien*, a Pi'ng-chau man, in A.D. 438 translated 13 books in 82 chapters, among which are—

1. Ch'uh-yau, the Dawn, or Coming forth of Light, being a copy of Dhammapada.

2. The History of Dharmavarddhana, the King's son, losing his eyes.

(2) The Shaman *Tan-mo-ye-she* (Dharmayasas), a Cophene man, translated in Canton, A.D. 399, 1 work in 1 chapter; also, A.D. 413, at Chang'an, 2 other works in 45 chapters.

(3) The Shaman Kumārajiva, originally a man of India, but afterwards of Karashar, was brought to China, and in A.D. 401 translated at Chang'an 98 books in 421 chapters.

(4) The Shaman *Fo-to-ye-she* (Brightness of Wisdom), a Cophene man, came to China and settled at Chang'an; he was called the Red-haired Vibasha (Barbarian), whilst his master, Kumārajiva, was called the Great Vibasha (Barbarian); he translated from A.D. 402 to A.D. 412 altogether 4 works in 69 chapters.

(5) The Shaman *Fo-ye-to-lo* (Punyatara), a Cophene man, resided in China A.D. 403, and translated the Vinaya according to the school of the Sarvâstavâdins, 1 book, 58 chapters.

(6) The Shaman *Fă-kin* translated 14 books in 18 chapters.

(7) The Shaman *Shih-tan-hioh*, otherwise called Hwei-hioh, obtained in Khoten an original of the work *Kin-u-king* (Sûtra of the Wise and Foolish), and in the year A.D. 409 translated it in 15 chapters.

(8) The Shaman *Shih-tan-yen*, a priest of the Tung-loh Temple at Hiuen-'an (in the Stony Grot); he became a disciple at an early age. The Emperor T'ai-wu-ti having persecuted the Buddhists, afterwards fell sick and became a convert, and in A.D. 452, Wen Chêng having ascended the throne, Tan continued to translate books till A.D. 463, with some Indian priests located in Stony Grot Temple. He produced altogether 2 works in 5 chapters.

(9) The Shaman *Kih-kia-ye* (Kakaya), a man of the west, travelled about on the work of conversion; he came to China in the second year of the period Yen-hing of the reign of Hiao-Wen-ti (A.D. 473), and translated 5 books in 25 chapters.

The Northern Liang (in Kansuh), of the Family Tsü K'ü.
[Capital, Ku-tsang.]

(1) The Shaman *Shih-tao-kung* came to Kansuh (North Liang) in *Ho-si* (Tangut) in the Yung-cho year of Wang-shin, and translated in Chang-yeh for the sake of Mung-Sun, king of Ho-si, 2 books in 12 chapters.

(2) The Shaman *Fă-chung*, a man of the Kao-chang district (Turfan), came to Chang-yeh at the same time, and also translated for Mung-Sun 1 book in 4 chapters.

(3) The Shaman *Săng-kia-to*, a man of the west, also, at the same time and place, and for Mung-Sun, translated 1 book in 2 chapters.

(4) The Shaman *Tan-mo-tsien* (Dharmâkshaya), a man of Mid-India, became a disciple at six years of age, and daily recited 10,000 words of Scripture. At first he belonged to the school of the Lesser Development, and was well acquainted with all the discourses of the five Vidyas. Afterwards meeting with a contemplative priest (Shan-sse) named Pih-teou, he became, after ten days' discussion with him, a follower of the Great Development school. He came to Ku-tsang (North Liang) in the year 412 A.D., bringing with him a copy of 10 chapters of the first division of the Nirvâna Sûtra, and also a copy of the Rules of the Bodhisatwas. The king (Sün) having heard of Dharmâkshaya, invited him to come and translate books, on which from the year 414 A.D. down to 421 A.D. he engaged in the task, and produced translations of 23 books in 148 chapters. Among these were—

1. Fo-pen-hing-king (a Life of Buddha by Asvaghosha Bodhisatwa), in 5 chapters.

2. Kin-kwong-ming-king (Suvarna Prabhâsa Sûtra), in 4 chapters.

3. Leng-kia-king (Lankâvatara Sûtra), in 4 chapters.

Afterwards he translated in the Hiao-kien year of Hiao-wu-ti of the Sung dynasty (house of Liu), A.D. 454, 35 books in 42 chapters. Among these are—

1. Kwan-si-yin-king, in 1 chapter.

2. Fo-mu-pan-ni-pan-king, in 1 chapter (the Death of the Mother of Buddha, *i.e.*, of Mahaprajâpati).

(5) The Shaman Buddhavarma, a man of the west, in the year 459 A.D. translated for the son of the king of Ho-si the Vibhasha Shastra, 1 book, 100 chapters. (Forty chapters were lost at the end of the Wei dynasty; sixty only now remain.)

(6) The Shaman *Shi-chi-mang* translated about the same time the Parinirvāna Sûtra in 20 chapters.

Other books, translators' names lost, belonging to this dynasty, 5 in number, in 17 chapters. Among these are—

1. Kin-kong-san-mui-king (the Vajra Samâdhi).
2. Kien-kih-wu-pih-fo-meng (Names of 500 Buddhas of the Bhadra Kalpa), 1 chapter.

The Sung Dynasty (*House of Liu*). [Capital, Kien K'ang.]

(1) The Shaman Buddhajiva, a man of Cophene (Cabul), became a disciple at an early age, and devoted himself to the study of the Vinaya of the Mahisasaka school. He came to the capital, Yang, in A.D. 423, and there having found the Vinaya Piṭaka of the Mahisasaka school, got by Fa-hien in Ceylon, the latter being now dead, the priests of the capital hearing that Jiva was well skilled in the Vinaya literature, begged him to translate this work. He therefore at the end of the year above named translated 34 chapters of it in the Lung Kwong Temple. He also translated one chapter of Religious Rules, and one chapter of Kamma Sañgha rules,[1] altogether 36 chapters. He was assisted in this work by the Shaman Chi-sheng of Khoten, who arranged the words, and by the Shaman Chu-tao-sing and others, who transcribed the written copy.

(2) The Shaman *Tan-mo-mi-to* (*i.e.*, a Dharmamita), a Cophene man; having made a vow to travel everywhere on the work of conversion, he came to China in 424 A.D., and translated 10 books in 14 chapters. [He painted a figure of Kapila.]

(3) The Shaman Kalayasas, a Western, came to China in 424 A.D., and translated 2 books in 2 chapters.

(4) The Shaman *I-yeh-po-lo* (Iśvara), a man of the west; he was well versed in the four Âgamas, and came to China in

[1] Rules made by a committee of priests, convoked on special occasions, *vide* Childers, Pâli Dict., *sub voc.* "Kammam," p. 178, col. 1.

the middle of the *Yuăn-kia* period of the reign of Wên-ti (about 438 A.D.), and translated the Samyuktabhidharmhṛidaya Sûtra, in 11 chapters.

(5) The Shaman *Sheh-chi-yan* of Liang-chau; he translated, A.D. 428—

1. P'hu-yaou-king, in 8 chapters.[1] In this he was assisted by Po-yun (Ratnamegha), one of Fa-hien's companions. This work was brought by Fa-hien from India, but he had not translated it.

2. Book of Jâtakas, in 5 chapters [Sing-king].

Altogether he translated 14 books in 36 chapters.

[It is related of this Shaman, that having broken one of the rules binding on a lay disciple, he was in doubt whether he could be ordained as a Shaman. In consequence he went by ship to India, and there consulted a Rahat. The Rahat, not being certain, consulted Maitreya (who was supposed to be in heaven). Maitreya having replied, "He may be ordained," Yăn was greatly rejoiced.]

(6) The Shaman Gunavarma, a man of Cophene, was a younger son of the king of that country; he was deeply versed in the nine Añgas,[2] in the four Âgamas, and in various sections of the Vinaya. He could recite more than a hundred myriad words of Scripture. He came to China about 440 A.D., and translated 8 books in 39 chapters.

(7) The Shaman *Po-yun*,[3] a Liang-chau man; he became a disciple when a child. He travelled across the Raksha desert to gaze on the sacred traces (A.D. 402). Whilst thus travelling he heard the sound of heavenly drums; he paid reverence to the traces of Sâkya; received the words of a Rahat, and after travelling through various countries, and practising himself in the letters and sounds of the Fan language, he came to Chang'an, and engaged with Chi-yan in the work of translation. Afterwards by himself, about the year 440 A.D., he translated—

1. Fo-pen-hing-tsan-king, in five[4] chapters [Life of Buddha in verse].

---

1 The second translation of the Lalita Vistara.

2 The Navañgam, *vide* Childers, *sub* "Añgam."

3 *Vide supra*, under No. 5. He was a man of *Western* Liang-chau.

4 This work, as it is before me, is in *seven* chapters.

2. Wou-liang-sheu-king, 2 chapters [Amitâyus Sûtra]. Altogether he translated 4 books in 22 chapters.

(8) The Shaman Sanghavarma, a man of India; he translated in 434 A.D., in China, in the Chang-tsin Temple, 5 books in 27 chapters. Among them—

1. The Abhidharma Vibhaśa, in 14 chapters.

2. The Mâtrika rules of the Vinaya according to the Sarvâstavâdin school.

3. The Verses of Nagarjuna exhorting the King, 1 vol.

(9) The Shaman Gunabhadra, a man of Mid-India, at an early age was an adept in the five Vidyas and the four Vedas; afterwards became a convert to Buddhism, and arrived in China in the year 436 A.D. He translated in the Chi-yuen (Jeta-vana) Temple of the capital till A.D. 444, altogether 78 books in 161 chapters.

[This priest being about to translate the Avatamsaka Sûtra, and fearing he had not sufficient knowledge of Chinese, prayed to Kwan-yin, on which he had a dream. He saw a man in white clothing approach him with a drawn sword in one hand and a man's head in the other. Approaching to Bhadra he said, "What troubles you!" On receiving his answer he added, "This need not concern you so much." On which, approaching him, he changed his head for the one in his hand, and said, "Have you experienced much pain?" on which Bhadra replied, "Not much." He then awoke.]

(10) The Shaman Dharmavīra[1] (Strength of the Law); his family name was Wai, a man of Hwang-Lung in Yu-chau; he became a Shami when young, and incited by the account of Fa-hien's personal travels, he vowed in the *Yung-ch'u* year of Wu-ti of the Sung dynasty, 420 A.D., to travel with some others of like mind, twenty-five men in all. After wandering through various countries for twenty years and more, he alone survived, and returned to Cophene, whence, having got some Sanscrit texts, he returned to China, and in the last year of the *Yuăn-kia* period (A.D. 453) he reached the capital, and there himself translated the Kwan-si-yen-shau-ki (Prophecy respecting Kwan Yin), in 1 chapter.

[1] In Chinese, *Fă-yung*.

(11) The Shaman *Shih-hwei-kan*, in the year 457 A.D., translated 25 books in 25 chapters. Among these are—

1. The Story of the person in Sravasti who went mad on the death of his son.
2. Pi-u-king (the Avadâna Sûtra).
3. The Parinirvâna of Buddha's Mother.
4. Kiu-tan-ni-king (Gotamî Sûtra).

(12) The Shaman *Kung-tih-chi* (Gunasatya ?), a man of the west, came to King-chau in China[1] A.D. 463, and translated 2 works in 7 chapters.

(13) The Shaman *Chu-fă-ch'uen*, an Indian, translated in Kwang-chau (Canton) in the T'ai-shih year of Ming-ti (465 A.D. . . . 472 A.D.) 6 works in 29 chapters.

(14) The Shaman *Shih-shoh-kung* translated at Nanhäe 1 work in 2 chapters.

(15) The Shaman *Shih-tao-yau* translated 2 works in 3 chapters.

(16) The Shaman *Shih-yung-kung* translated 4 books in 4 chapters.

(17) The Shaman *Shih-fă-hae* translated 2 works in 2 chapters.

(18) The Shaman *Shih-sien-kung* translated 1 work (the Chandradipa Samâdhi) in 1 chapter.

The Tsi Dynasty, the Family of Su. [Capital, Kien K'ang.]

(1) The Shaman *Tan-mo-kia-to-ye-she* (Dharmajâtayasas), a man of India, came to Canton in the third year of the period Kien Yuän (A.D. 482), and translated 1 work in 1 chapter, viz., the *Won-liang-i-king*.

(2) The Shaman *Mo-ho-shing* (Mahayâna) came to China from the west about 490 A.D., and translated in Canton 1 work in 1 chapter, viz., Wu-pih-pen-sing-king (the 500 Jâtakas).

(3) The Shaman Sanghabhadra came from the west, bent on the work of conversion, in A.D. 489, and with the Shaman Săng-i translated in Canton, in the Chuh-lin Temple, 1 work in 18 chapters.

(4) The Shaman Dharmamati, a man of the west, came to

[1] In *Hupeh*.

China 491 A.D., and translated in Yang-chau 2 works in 13 chapters, one of which is the Devadatta section of the Sad-dharma Pundarika.

(5) The Shaman Gunavati, a man of Mid-India, came to Yang-chau, and translated in the year 493 A.D. 3 works in 12 chapters. Of these—

1. The Sûtra of the Twelve Nidânas.
2. The Sûtra of the Householder Sudatta.

(6) The Shaman *Shih-fă-to* came to China and translated in Yang-chau 2 works in 2 chapters.

(7) The Shaman *Shih-tan-king* translated 2 works in 4 chapters. Of these, *Mo-ho-ma-ye-king* (the Sûtra of Maha-mâya).

(8) The Shaman *Shih-fa-ni* translated 1 work in 2 chapters.

The Dynasty of the Southern Wei, Family of Yuän.

[Capital, Loyang.]

(1) The Shaman Dharmaruchi, a man of South India, an adept in the interpretation of the Vinaya Piṭaka. Wẹll affected to the world, he came to Loyang on his travels A.D. 502, and translated one work in 5 chapters. Again, in the year 504 A.D., he translated one work in 1 chapter.

(2) The Shaman *Shih-fă-ch'ang*, a man of the Yuän-wei, translated one work in Loyang, 1 chapter.

(3) The Shaman Bodhiruchi, a man of North India, an adept in the Dhâraṇî Scriptures, and well versed in the three Piṭakas, came to Loyang in 508 A.D., and there, in the Yung-ning Temple, with seven hundred other Indian priests, translated the Dasabhumi Sûtra. Afterwards he translated 39 books in 127 chapters. Among these—

1. The Lankâvatara Sûtra, 10 chapters.
2. Fă-tsah-king.
3. The Vâjra-prâjna-paramita Sûtra, 1 chapter.
4. Kia-ye-shan-teng-king (Gayâ-sirsha Sûtra).
5. An index of Sûtras and Shastras translated.

(4) The Shaman *Le-na-mo-ti* (Ratnamati), also called Po-ti (Bodhi), a man of Mid-India, able to recite 100,000 gâthas. Bent on teaching, he travelled here and there, and came to

China in 508 A.D., and translated in Loyang 5 books in 23 chapters.

(5) The Shaman Buddhasanda, a man of North India, of profound intellect, came to China A.D. 525, and worked at translations till A.D. 538 in Loyang in the White Horse Temple, and also in Linchang (Nieh To) in the Kin-fa (Golden Flower) Temple. In all, he translated 10 books in 11 chapters.

The Liang Dynasty, Family of Su. [Capital, Kien K'ang.]

(1) The Shaman Maṇḍala (or Mandâra), a man of Funan (Cambodia), came to China A.D. 504, and translated with Sanghapalita in the capital Yang, three works, 11 chapters.

(2) The Shaman Sanghapalita or Sanghavarma, a man of Funan, came to China A.D. 502, and translated in three different places 11 books in 38 chapters. Among these are—

1. Aśokarâja Sûtra in 10 chapters.
2. The Prâjnaparamita Sûtra of Manjusri.

(3) The Shaman Paramita, also called Gunarata (?), a man of Western India, of Ujjein, came to China A.D. 549, and translated, at the instigation of the king, till 555 A.D., in the Ching Kwan Temple and elsewhere, 10 books in 20 chapters. Between A.D. 557 and A.D. 569 he translated in Canton, with the others, 50 books in 149 chapters.

The Eastern Wei Dynasty, the Family of Yuän.
[Capital, K'ang Nieh.]

The Upasaka Gotamaprajñaruchi, a man of South India, born in Benares, of the Brahman caste, applied himself when young to Buddhist studies, came to China A.D. 538, and till A.D. 542 translated in the capital 14 books in 85 chapters. Among these are—

1. Ching-fă-nien-chu-king in 70 vols. (Saddharma smriti upasthâna Sûtra).
2. Kin-sih-wang-king (Suvarṇa Râja Sûtra).

The T'si Dynasty (Northern T'si), the Family of Kao.
[Capital, Nieh.]

The Shaman Nalandayasas, a man of North India, of the

country of Udyâna. He became a disciple at an early age, and travelled as a pilgrim to the various sacred spots of his religion, and at last came to China, A.D. 558, and until A.D. 569 translated with Dharmadana in the capital 7 books, 52 chapters. Afterwards he translated 8 other books in 20 chapters.

The Ch'ên Dynasty, Family of Ch'ên. [Same Capital.]

The son of the king of the country of Ujjein, named Upasena (or Upasunya), translated in China from A.D. 538 to A.D. 541, 3 books, 7 chapters. He afterwards, A.D. 566, translated another work in 7 chapters.

The Chow Dynasty. [Capital, Chang'an.]

(1) The Shaman Jnañabhadra, a man of the Po-teou-mo (Paduma ?) country, came to Chang'an in the reign of Meng-ti (A.D. 557–561), and there translated the Panchavidya Shastra in 1 chapter.

(2) The Shaman Jnañayasas, a man of Magadha (with his two disciples Yasa-kûta and Jnaña-kûta), came to China A.D. 565, and till A.D. 572 translated at Chang'an 6 books in 17 chapters.

(3) The Shaman Yasa-kûta, a man of Udyâna, with his companion Jnaña-kûta, translated during the reign of Wu-ti (A.D. 561–578) in various temples 4 books in 9 chapters.

(4) The Shaman Jnaña-kûta, a man of Gandhâra in North India, of the Kshatriya caste, became a disciple when young, and travelled about teaching and converting, came to the borders of Ta-sse, and afterwards in the reign of Wu-ti translated 4 books in 5 chapters. Again, in the Sui dynasty, A.D. 588 till A.D. 596, he translated 33 books in 154 chapters. Among these, Fo-pen-hing-tsi-king, in 60 chapters.[1]

(5) Dharmaprâjna, a Brahman, came to China in 583 A.D., translated 1 book in 1 chapter.

(6) The Shaman Panitaruchi (or Vinataruchi), a man of Udyâna, in North India, translated in 583 A.D. 2 books in 2 chapters.

(7) The Shaman Dharmagupta, of South India, came to China 591 A.D., and translated 18 books in 81 chapters.

[1] Partly translated into English, as the "Romantic History of Buddha."

The Great Tang Dynasty, the Family of Wai.
[Capital, Chang'an.]

(1) The Shaman Prabhakala or Prabha, of Mid-India, of the Kshatriya race, came to China, in pursuance of his vow to travel everywhere for the purpose of teaching, in the first year of the *Chêng Kwan* period, A.D. 627, and in the Ta-hing-shan Temple translated 3 books in 13 chapters.

(2) The Shaman Hiouen Thsang, a man of Loyang, his family name Chen, travelled through India, and translated altogether 75 works in 1235 chapters.

(3) The Shaman *Shih-i-tsing*,[1] a man of Ts'i-chan.[2] His family name was Chang, his private name was Wen. He became a disciple when very young, and at fifteen years of age resolved to visit the Western world, like the unpretending Fa-hien or the famous Hiouen Thsang; and so, in the second year of *Hien Hêng* (A.D. 671–672), he came with thirty-seven others to Kwang-fu (Canton), and out of these, ten embarked with him on his travels, but these all got away from the ship and left him alone. And so with earnest resolve and unattended he went on, and after many dangers and delays came to the borders of India. He studied the languages of all the countries he passed through. Deeply he reverenced the sacred spots on the Vulture Peak and the Cock-foot Mount; gladly he advanced to the Jetavana and the Deer Park, and then, taking a circuit, rested in the Nâlanda College and worshipped at the Bo-Tree. He studied, under eminent masters, both the Little and Great Vehicle. After visiting more than thirty countries, he returned homewards, having been away some twenty years, and arriving at the River Loh (in Honan, a tributary of the Yellow River), [he disembarked]. He brought home with him nearly four hundred distinct volumes of original copies of the Sûtra, Vinaya, and Abidharma (scriptures), comprising 500,000 verses. He also brought one picture of the Diamond Throne and three hundred fragments of *sariras* (body-relics). The Heavenly Queen (*Tin-hau* or *Wu-hau*, the empress), in her reverence for

[1] This is the celebrated priest, *I-Tsing*.
[2] A part of Shantung, east of T'ai-shan.

religion (the law), accompanied by her family friends, went forth from the eastern gate to meet him and his sacred treasure. His dark-clad companions bore flags; music was heard on every side as he advanced to the Shan-ki Temple. Here he rested and began his work of translation. During the years 700–703 A.D. he translated, first with (a priest) of Khoten, and afterwards by himself, in the Fuh-sien Temple of the Eastern capital, or in the Sai-ming Temple of the Western capital, the following works (twenty in number).[1] Afterwards, in the first year of the *Shên Lung* cycle (705), he translated at the Eastern capital in the inner precinct the following work in three chapters, "The Chant of the Peacock-râja" (*Mayūra rāja dhāranī*), and in the Ta-fuh-sien Temple three other works.

Altogether, from the first year of the cycle *Kin-she* (under the rule of the Empress *Wu*) till the second year of the cycle *King-Yün* (under the rule of the Emperor Jui Tsung) [700 A.D. to 712 A.D.], he (with others co-operating) translated fifty-six distinct treatises (*P'o*), including altogether 230 chapters (*kiouen*).

The North Indian priest Anîjana and the priest Dharmamatma of Turkhâra explained the original meaning of the Fan (Sanscrit or Prakrit); the priest Dharmananda of Cophene (Cabul) and the layman (grihapati) of East India, Sringishra (?), with others, explained the Fan letters; the Shaman Hṛimati and others read the Fan original; the layman Gotamavājra, of Eastern India, the Prince Arjun of Cashmere, and others, translated (from the words thus rendered); the Shaman Po-lun and others wrote down the translation, whilst others revised what was written. Various dukes and officers received the translations when completed and presented them to the emperor.

Besides the above, there were compiled, either before or after, the following:—

Tai-tang-si-u-kiu-fă-kao-săng-ch'uen, 1 volume, 2 chapters.

Tai-tang-nan-hai-k'i-kwei-niu-fă-chu'en, 1 volume, 4 chapters, and 3 others, altogether 5 books, 9 chapters.

He was engaged about an edition of the Sarvastivadinvastu

[1] Names omitted.

when he attained Nirvâna, having written out 70 or 80 chapters of the original. Besides all these there were others, such as the *Makara-Fish* Sûtra, &c., amounting to 49 chapters, which were left unfinished.

Referring to the foregoing records, I desire to call your notice to the earnest work of these Buddhist missionaries in China. By sheer dint of labour they produced a new literature in that country. Not only so, but they covered the land with Temples and Pagodas, which exist to the present day. They invented a syllabic mode of spelling, which is still used and found of great value. More than this, they revolutionised the religious thought of the empire, and led the way for the diffusion of the knowledge of their books throughout Japan, Corea, and Mongolia. What was the secret of their success? One reason, at least, is to be found in the grandeur and simplicity of Buddha's teaching. Grand, because it grasped the idea, however imperfectly, of a universal Saviour; simple, because it laid the foundation in self-denial—self-denial without *self* in it. The term "*wou wei*" in Chinese—and this term is used as synoptic of the ethical teaching of Buddha—signifies "absence of self." In the first of the *Forty-two Sections* Buddha says that "*he* is rightly called a Shaman who is able to exhibit in his conduct this 'absence of self'" (*wou wei*). M. Leon Feer translates this phrase "*le principe de la noncomposition.*" Mr. Edkins renders it "*non-action;*" but its real meaning is only to be got at by careful comparison. For instance, we have the same term used in this sentence, "*Wou wei i chi ché, ki Shun ye yu,*" *i.e.*, "He who without thought of self yet governs (himself), he is indeed like Shun." And again, respecting Laou Tseu, it is said, "*Shang teh wou wei i wou i wei,*" "The highest virtue is to act without thought of self, without knowing it;" on which the gloss is, "*Wou yeou sin u teh,*" "They think not that they are virtuous," or, as M. Stas. Julien[1] renders it, "They practise virtue, naturally." Again there is another sentence, "*Ngai min chi kwoh neng wou wei,*" "Loving the people, governing the

[1] Syntaxe Nouvelle Monographies, p. 112.

country well, this man will attain freedom from self," *i.e.*, will be able to act without any feeling of selfish desire.

These passages from secular books confirm the sense of the phrase used in Buddhist works, and explain how this very phrase is employed as a synonym for Nirvâna, that condition of freedom which, in fact, consists in a freedom from *self.* This is the highest bliss, and on this simple truth Buddhism is to a great extent founded.

I will conclude this Lecture by the translation of a Jātaka, or Birth-story; it is known as the Śivi Jātaka, and is frequently referred to as an example of the principle of self-sacrifice of which I have spoken. There is an allusion to it, Pl. lx. of Mr. Fergusson's "Tree and Serpent Worship."

The Śivi Jātaka,

As it is related in the *Ta-chwang-yan-King-Lun*,[1] k. xii., fol. 1-11.

Text or Subject.

Once more; it is no easy thing to get to hear the law of Buddha. In old time when Tathágata was a Bodhisatwa, he did not spare his own body (life) in seeking after the law (*i.e.*, in seeking to fulfil the law). We ought therefore to use all diligence in listening to the law.

I heard in time past the following story (comparison or avadâna) of the Pigeon. There was a certain heretical teacher who recited for the instruction of Śâkradevendra a religious code of instruction (law), subversive of the true law. Now, that heretical teacher, having no true knowledge, called himself the All-wise, and he said there was no such thing as the condition called "Anuttara samyak sambhodi." At this time the Divine Sâkra, having heard his words, was heavy at heart, and ill content. Whereupon, looking through all the world, he

[1] This work was written by Asvaghosha, and will be referred to hereafter. It may perhaps be restored to *Mahālamkara Sûtra Shastra.*

examined the cases of those who were undergoing austerities, to see whether any of them had arrived at the condition at which they aimed, viz., complete wisdom. And so the Gâtha says, in the "Sûtra of the Questions of the Divine Sâkra"—

"My mind is now occupied in anxious search (inquiry),
And I am unable to find a sufficient answer.
Morning and night I am disturbed with painful doubt,
Not knowing whether this matter is so or not.
And now I have come from far,
Anxious and earnest in my wide-spreading search,
Not knowing where at present dwells the man
Who has accomplished the great experiment."

Then Visvakarman addressed the divine Sâkra and said, "He who dwells in heaven above should not give way to grief and heaviness. There is in the country of Ku-shi a king named Shi-pi (Śivi), persevering in his austerities, engaged in seeking supreme wisdom. According to the opinion of those who have investigated the case, this king will ere long arrive at the condition of a Buddha. Let us go and observe for ourselves." The divine Sâkra answered, "Yes! but he may give up his aim, may he not?" And so the Gâtha says—

"Even as the fish produces much spawn,
Though little of it comes to perfection,
Or as the Amra fruit
When fully ripe is difficult to distinguish,[1]
So is it with the Bodhisatwa.
Those who engage in high resolves are many,
But few are those who accomplish their aim.
If in the practice of painful austerities
He allows not his mind to vacillate or change,
He may be called 'one who has attained fixity.'
Those who desire to know (or to be) a true Bodhisatwa
Must test this unchangeable strength of heart."

Visvakarman then said, "Let us go, then, and examine into this case, and see if there is any vacillation; and if not, then let us present our offerings in honour of the recluse."

On this the divine Sâkra, from a wish to investigate the

[1] Or, As it is difficult to find a *ripe* Amra fruit, &c.

mind (heart) of the Bodhisatwa, transformed himself into a hawk, and bade Visvakarman change himself into a dove. Then Visvakarman, having assumed this form, its body blue as the ether, its eyes like vermilion gems, came flying down to the place where the divine Sâkra was. At this time the divine Sâkra, conceiving much pity in his heart, addressed Visvakarman, and said, "How can we find it in our heart to add to the sorrow of Bodhisatwa? Yet, though we do increase for a time the pain of this Sivirâja, yet it is but as the jeweller who tries the true gem by piercing it, and chipping it, holding it in the fire, and striking it. By these means he proves it to be a true gem." (So in the present case.)

And now the dove, because it was pursued by the hawk, filled with fear in the presence of all beholders, sought refuge in the bosom of Sivirâja (or *under his shoulder*), its colour blue as the lotus leaf (here the colour *blue* is uncertain), and its brilliancy like the white beam of pure light that darts from the black cloud. Then all people seeing it were filled with awe, and said—

"He truly must have a loving heart,
For all things living place entire confidence in him.
As at the time of the sun's withdrawing her light,
Every bird repairs to its own nest.
But the hawk (transformed) addressed to him these words—
'Oh, king! I beg you give me back my food!'"

At this time the king (Mahârâja), having heard the words of the hawk, and seeing once more the extreme fright and alarm of the dove, replied forthwith in the following verses—

"Because the dove fears the hawk,
With fluttering pennons it comes to seek my protection;
Though it cannot speak with its mouth,
Yet through fear its eyes are filled with moisture.
I will now extend, therefore, (to this poor creature)
My protection and defence."

At this time the Mahârâja, to compose and pacify the trembling dove, added these verses—

"Fear not, give not way to alarm;
He shall not kill thee at the last.
Safe under my protection,
I will indeed defend thee from harm.
And why should I not save and deliver thee?
I, who design to save the world (all flesh),
I who, for the sake of all that lives,
Am now exerting such strength of purpose (ministering strength).
For even as those who receive the country's revenue,
For every six send one to me,
So now I, dwelling in the world
As a guest, receive this one,
Desiring to protect and defend it,
And not to suffer any calamity to befall it."

At this time the hawk answered the king thus, "Mahârâja, this dove is mine for food." The king replied, "But I have long conceived a loving heart towards all creatures, and therefore I ought to save and protect it." The hawk then asked the king, and said, "What mean you by this 'long time'?" Then the Mahârâja replied in these verses—

"When first I undertook to obtain wisdom (Bodhi),
At this time also I took on me to defend (the weak)
All living things of whatever sort,
Draw forth my compassion and my pity."

And then the hawk replied in these gâthas—

"If, then, your words be really true,
You ought, by right, to return me the dove;
For if I die from starvation,
How can you claim then 'a loving heart'?"

The king having heard these words, forthwith began to reflect: "I find myself, indeed, at present in a strait. I must cast over in my mind for some device by which to justify my conduct." Having thought thus, he straightway addressed the hawk, and said, "Will other flesh but this one's preserve your life?" He answered the king and said, "Yes! Fresh flesh with blood can save me alive." At this time the Mahârâja reflected thus—"What shall be done?" and then he said in verse—

"All living things, whatever sort they be,
I must ever defend from harm and contrive to protect;
But as for this matter of warm blood and flesh,
It cannot be had without some one's death."

Having thought thus, it occurred to him that it would be easy to give the hawk some flesh from his own body, and so he uttered the following verses—

"By cutting flesh from my own body,
And using it for satisfying the hawk,
I may thus let this one's body escape,
And protect him, trembling for his life."

At this time the Mahârâja, having repeated these verses, again addressed the hawk and said, "Will my flesh satisfy your hunger?" To which he replied, "If the king will give me of his flesh as much as the pigeon (in weight), then I will eat it (and live)." Then the Mahârâja, having heard these words, was filled with gladness, and addressed his servant, "Haste thee! bring the scales, and cut from my body flesh equal in weight to this dove. This is indeed a lucky day for me; how comes it that I am so fortunate?" And then he added these verses—

"(In this body of mine) dwell old age and disease,
Ever exposed to death and fragile, filled with loathsome
 humours;
Now for religion's sake
I will cut off this poor and corrupting flesh."

And then the servant of the king hastily brought the scales, whilst the Mahârâja, seeing them, without change of colour forthwith offered for mutilation his thigh, the white flesh of which was soft and moist as the Tâla leaf; and then calling his servant-man, he addressed him in these verses and said—

"Come now, with your knife
Cut off and take the flesh of my thigh.

Obey my words simply and faithfully,
And do not give way to anxious thought,
For then I shall not accomplish my object in suffering this pain,
Then I shall not obtain that highest wisdom I seek.
For of all kinds of wisdom
In the three worlds, this is the most excellent.
But this Bodhi by a single mischance
May not after all be obtained,
I am therefore now, on this account,
Most anxious to be firm and resolute as iron."

At this time the servant-man, his eyes filled with pitiful tears, with his hands clasped, addressed (the Râja) thus: "Pity me, gracious lord! I cannot do this deed. I have always obeyed and executed the orders of the king, but I cannot endure to cut the flesh off the thigh of the king with a knife." And then he repeated these verses—

"The king is he who saves and relieves (from unpleasant duties).
Were I to attempt to cut the king's flesh,
Myself, with the knife in my hand,
Would faint and fall down to earth."

At this time the Mahârâja in his own hand took the knife to cut off the flesh from his thigh. Then his great minister besought him not to commit such a deed, in vain. All the men in the city, his friends and relatives, the Brahmans, the women of the palace, raising their voices, in tears entreated him; the Devas, Nâgas, Yakshas, Gandharvas, Asuras, Kinnaras, Mahoragas, and so on, occupying space, cried one to another, "Such a thing as this was never heard of before!" At this time the Mahârâja encouraged himself in the following words—

"Psha! let my heart be established and fixed.
How light and trivial a pain is this!
Why then is my heart oppressed and sad?
See how many there are in the world
Entangled and held captive by innumerable sorrows,
Without refuge, without protection or defence,
With no covering (shelter), or support,

And unable to experience (or arrive at) any self-reliance !
But this heart of mine is otherwise placed.
There is deliverance and protection (for me);
Why then not blame myself
For thus entertaining the feeling of sorrow?"

Then Sâkradevendra thought thus: "This Mahârâja, will he be able to fix his heart or not in bearing the excessive pain?" And then he said, "Now you feel how difficult it is to bear such pain; you have had enough; let the bird go." Then Bodhisatwa, with a gentle smile on his face, replied, "Such pain is nothing. I swear that if I had to endure much greater pain, it should not prevent my purpose. And consider how small such pain as this is compared with that of hell. We ought to think of that, and raise a heartfelt love within, which may prompt us to deliver men from such misery." Having thought thus, he repeated the following verses—

"I now endure the pain consequent on this wound,
But how little this compared with that
Which those endure in hell!
So great, so lasting, and severe,
How can such pains as those be borne?
Now therefore I, in pity for such wretched ones,
Seek for a speedy rescue.
In gaining supreme wisdom
May I be able to save and deliver
From all such miseries."

Then the divine Sâkra thought with himself thus: "I ought to try whether the Mahârâja's heart will fail him if I remind him of greater pain than this he has to bear." Thinking thus, he still remained silent. Then the Mahârâja flung in the scales the one piece of flesh he had cut off, and in the other scale he placed the pigeon; but the body of the dove weighed down the other. Then cutting off a second piece from his other thigh, he placed it in the scale, but yet it was outweighed—and so with different parts of his body. Then the king, in doubt and fear as to what could be the cause of such a circumstance, raised himself with a view to place his body in the scale, on which the hawk rejoined, "Why are you moving? Do you repent of your purpose?" The Mahârajâ answered, "I repent not at all, but I desire to cast my entire body into the scale as a ransom for the dove!" At this time, when about thus to sacrifice his body, his face shone with joy, so that his friends on either side could not look at him, whilst others fled, not able to see him thus; whereupon the king called on them to behold him, and then piece by piece he cut his body joint from joint, even as a painted figure when placed in the falling rain is destroyed and effaced, and difficult to be recognised.

At this time the Mahârâja chanted forth these words—

"I now sacrifice my body, not for wealth, not for precious gems, not for any joys of sense, not for wife or child, not for house or friends or kin, but in the search after supreme wisdom by which to save the world (all flesh)." And then he repeated these lines—

"The Devas and Asuras,
The Gandharvas and Yakshas,
The Nâgas and Kwei-Shin (Spirits or Pretas),
All living things that exist
Who have seen this body of mine,
All may know that I turn not back
In my desire after the attainment of wisdom.
Though my body is racked and cut to pieces,
Those who seek to plant the seeds of knowledge
Ought above all things to have a firm, loving heart.
If they be not fixed and true to their purpose,
Then they will lose the prize of wisdom they seek for."

Then the Mahârâja, not sparing his own life, forthwith placed himself in the scales. Then the great earth shook six times, as when grass or leaves are driven here and there by the tempest; and then in the midst of space the assembled Devas, murmuring their applause at such an unwonted sight, exclaimed, "Well done! well done! this is rightly called indomitable perseverance (virya), firm and unmoved in purpose indeed!" And then he added the words of the Gâthas—

"Because I would protect that life,
I myself have lacerated this flesh of mine;

With sincere purpose cultivating a pitiful and loving heart,
Firm in my resolution and not to be shaken.
All the assembled Devas
Have experienced unusual thoughts."

At this time the hawk (as he appeared) murmured forth his surprise at the unheard-of spectacle, and said, "Not long hence this man, so firm in his purpose, will arrive at perfect intelligence (Buddha), to whom all men will look as to their loving parents." Then Sâkra resumed his right appearance before the king, and, telling Visvakarman also to resume his, he added, "Now we both must present our offerings to this Bodhisatwa, so strong in his purpose; even as Mount Sumeru, firmly fixed in the midst of the ocean, can never be shaken, so also is the heart of this Bodhisatwa." And then they added these gâthas—

"We ought indeed to present our offerings
To this courageous and resolute one;
We ought now together to sing aloud
His praises and extol him greatly.
All those oppressed by fear of danger or trouble
Ought to seek in him protection and be at rest,
With him to form a close alliance,
Who for so long has resolutely prepared himself,
And laid the foundation of a great merciful heart.
All the wise should seek shelter
Beneath the branches and boughs which now appear
Growing from this tree of perfect wisdom."

Then Visvakarman, addressing the divine Sâkra, said: "Now, Mahârâja, we ought from pity to all that lives to restore his body as it was before, and express a strong desire that the wisdom-heart of all creatures may not change." Then divine Sâkra inquired of the king and said, "And did you not repent of your purpose to give your life for the sake of that single dove?" At this time the Mâhâraja said in verses—

"This body of mine must return to nothingness,
Even as yonder piece of wood or stone,
Devoured either by brute beasts,
Burnt with fire, or rotting in the ground.

But yet this body of such little worth
Is made the means of producing great advantage,
And so my heart is filled with joy,
And there is no repentance found with me.
Who is there possessing wisdom
But will greatly rejoice to feel
That with this vile and stricken body
Such universal benefit by firmness may accrue?"

Then divine Sâkra added this question, "These words are indeed difficult to believe." And then he added, "Is it true indeed as you say?" On this the Mahârâja made this vow (*sacha kiriya*), "If my heart felt no sorrow or regret" (*i.e., in proof* that it felt none), "let my body return to its perfect form and be as it was." And then the Mahârâja, having considered his body, mangled as it was, said as follows—

"At the time when I cut the flesh off my body,
My heart felt no sorrow or regret,
No resentment and no disappointment;
My heart had no feeling but joy.
If this is true as I say,
Then my body should return to its old state,
And I soon shall attain the way of Bodhi,
And save all living things from pain."

Having uttered these words, the mangled body of the Mahârâja was restored whole as at first, and then he uttered these words—

"All the mountains and the great earth
Were shaken and moved;
The trees and the great ocean
Were disturbed and in commotion, unable to rest,
As those who tremble with fear,
Or those who join in battle are in turmoil.
All the Devas sang their hymns,
And from space there fell perfumes and flowers;
All sounds of music were heard,
The host of Devas raised their voices,
They sang in joyous strain
And recited their tuneful verses.

Then all creatures were greatly moved;
The great ocean uttered its voice,
The heavens rained down the finest perfumed rice,
And filled completely all the ways
The flowers which fell from space;
Some descended fast and others slowly.
All the Devas in the air
Covered the earth with flowers of every kind
And of every gaudy colour.
Gold and jewels, ornaments and garments,
Came down from heaven like rain.
The garments of the Devas
As they touched each other produced a sound.
In all the abodes of men
Precious vessels of themselves appeared;
And as they shone in the various chambers,
Of themselves emitted sounds
Like the music of the Apsaras.
No clouds were spread above the world,
But all the regions of space were clear and still;
A gentle breeze breathed perfumed air,
The rivers flowed with quiet murmur;
The Yakshas all desired to act religiously,
And to cause increase and benefit to men.
Not long hence I shall accomplish perfect wisdom,
And hence the songs and hence the praises.
My heart is therefore filled with joy,
Whilst all the Gandharvas
Sound forth their hymns and music
In light and sonorous strains,
And this the burthen of their songs:
'Not long hence he shall be a perfect Buddha,
And by his mighty vow cross o'er the sea
And bring deliverance to the distressed.
Oh! when he has obtained his aim
May he remember to deliver us.'"

Then divine Sâkra and Visvakarman, having made their offerings, returned to their heavenly palaces.

And now to conclude. I have stated that the majority of Buddhist Books known in the South may be found in China.

Let us consider the statement. The Buddhist Books written in Pāli and composing the Southern Canon were taken to Ceylon, at different periods, from Kalinga, Andhra, and the neighbourhood (*Oldenberg*). Probably they were all so taken before the Christian era. These books were reproduced in Pāli by Buddhaghosha about A.D. 400. Now the same works must have been known throughout India at least as early as Aśoka, for the Canon was supposed to be then in existence. Is it to be supposed that they were everywhere written or known in the Magadhī language (Pāli)? Such a supposition is improbable on the face of it. There were vernaculars (*bashyas*) everywhere, and there were Buddhists everywhere in India. We argue, therefore, that these books, when written, were written not in Ceylon only in Pāli, but everywhere in that tongue where they were accepted, and from these tongues they were translated into Chinese. The Cophene priests were evidently the most diligent in translating their Scriptures in China; they brought texts with them, but not Pāli texts, yet texts of the same Scriptures. And therefore we doubt not the recognised books of the South will, with few exceptions, be found in the North (so far at least as they were *Indian*), and as far as we have yet searched, this fact has been established.

But to show this the better I must ask your attention to my next Lecture.

LECTURE II.

ON THE METHOD OF BUDDHA'S TEACHING AS EXHIBITED IN THE VINAYA PITAKA.

A CONSENSUS of opinion gathered from books recently published tends to show, without much room for question, that the translations of the Sacred Books of the Buddhists made in India, probably between the time of Aśoka and the first century B.C., were written (if written at all, and not merely handed down traditionally), not in the languages known as Sanscrit and Pāli only, but in various dialects, according to the locality in which the books were first framed. This is an important step to have made in our knowledge of the subject, because it removes us at once from the arena of a controversy which formerly tied us to considerations of a preliminary character—I mean the controversy with regard to the comparative antiquity of the two supposed versions of the Canon, viz., that in Pāli and that in Sanşcrit. It is well known that Mr. Brian Hodgson, who may be rightly considered as the discoverer of Northern Buddhism, was, and we believe is, an advocate for the priority of the Sanscrit version of the Buddhist Sacred Scriptures. His language is very definite: "The philosophic founders of Buddhism used Sanscrit, and Sanscrit only, to expound, defend, and record the speculative principles of their religion" (*Journ. As. Soc. of Bengal*, vol. vi. p. 683). At the same time he allowed that in the actual propagandism of their religion the teachers used popular idioms, but yet the philosophic ideas which formed, as it were, the basis of their teaching were preserved from the earliest period in Sanscrit. So, at least, I understand his words; and in proof or confirmation of this opinion he refers to the absence of such works as the Prajña-paramitā in the so-called Southern school, which adopted the Pāli as its sacred language. Following Hodgson, we have a list of eminent writers on this subject who hold to the view of two canonical versions only. Lassen supposes that from the first Buddha addressed the Brahmans in Sanscrit, and the people in Magadhî or Pāli, and he assumes that two versions of the Canon existed from the time of the first council, viz., one in Sanscrit and the other in Pāli, whilst those Sûtras which were not produced till a much later time, viz., about the period of Kanishka, were compiled in popular idioms in districts where Sanscrit was but ill understood, such as in Kashmir. Burnouf, also, admitting two versions or redactions of the Buddhist Scriptures, assumes that one was designed for the people and the other for the learned Brahmans; but in the case of the Pāli version he thinks that it was reduced to its present form later than the Sanscrit, as it was more and more affected by grammatical influences from without. Mr. D'Alwis considers the Pāli as the orthodox Buddhist language, whilst he regards the Nepalese Sanscrit Books as the product of an heretical movement, noticed in the Ceylonese Chronicles, and particularly the *Dipavamsa.* The late Professor Childers, as is well known, upheld the sacred character of the Pāli, as the language of the texts; "he cannot conceive how any one can believe the Pāli books to be translations from the Sanscrit;" and he states his own view to be, "that the North Buddhist Sanscrit texts are founded on older Pāli texts—the texts, in fact, of Southern Buddhism, of which they are in some cases in great part literal translations."

In opposition to this opinion of only two redactions of the Canon, Mr. Minayef, in his introduction to his Pāli Grammar, has shown that there were probably various versions of Buddha's teaching, handed down orally in different localities. His words are these: "It is difficult not to conclude, from what has been said, that there were not originally only two redactions of Buddha's teaching, comprising one Canon only, but that the primitive literature transmitted orally was modified according to the language of each country." It is true that in forming this conclusion he rests very much on a text, which, according to Childers, he has misunderstood, and which would rather strengthen the views of the latter scholar as to the sacred character (and its exclusive use in Buddhist writings) of the Pāli. Yet, omitting this, there are other considerations of considerable weight which seem to confirm his argument. Of these, the most important he derives from an examination of the Aśoka rock-cut edicts, which furnish us with specimens of various dialects of India, all differing from the Pāli:—1. The dialect of Western India, as embodied in the Girnar inscription; 2. the dialect of North-West India, as found in the Kapur de Giri inscription; 3. the dialect of Eastern India, as found in the inscriptions of Dhauli; and 4. the Lat inscriptions. All of these distinguish themselves from Pāli, principally in their phonetical character, *e.g.*, there are no consonantal reduplications, which occur in Pāli, as in the word *Sadhamme* for *saddhame*, *sute* for *sutta*. It is curious again to observe that the word *Samgha* is used in the Bhabra inscription instead of the Pāli *Sangha;* the letter *l* is substituted for *r*, as *lāja* for *rājā*, *āliya* for *āriya;* and again, we find the neuter singular in *e* instead of *a;* from all which Minayef concludes that the Pāli is "clearly distinguished from all the dialects of these inscriptions." If this be so, it is questionable how far the assertion that the Sanscrit versions of the Buddhist Books were made from Pāli only can be sustained; it would rather seem probable that there existed in India, after the use of writing became general, copies of these books in various dialects, and that the later Sanscrit versions were made not from *one* redaction only, but from such copies as happened to be in possession of the Pandits in Nepal, by whom these translations were made.

This question of the origin and right place of the Pāli language has been discussed lately in the valuable introduction to Dr. Oldenberg's edition of the Mahâvagga section of the Vinaya Piṭaka. He asks (p. xlix), "To what part of India did the Pāli originally belong, and from whence did it spread to Ceylon?" The answer to this question, he adds, may be reached either from an historical investigation as to the road by which the sacred writings were carried to Ceylon, or, secondly, on the basis of the ancient inscriptions, by inquiry to what geographical limits the grammatical peculiarities which distinguish the Pāli from other dialects of India are confined. With regard to the first, Dr. Oldenberg remarks that Westergaard and E. Kuhn have assumed that because Mahinda, the son of Aśoka, lived at Ujjenî till he was ten years old, that the language he made use of when he went as a missionary to Ceylon was that of Ujjenî (Udyâna). This he regards as very improbable, in consideration of the fact that Mahinda resided at the court at Pâṭaliputra ten years before he joined the Buddhist Sañgha, and it is hardly probable that he studied the sacred books or learned the sacred traditions in the dialect of Ujjenî when he lived in the district of its earliest development. And again he remarks, that though we are not acquainted with the exact character of the Ujjenî dialect from any inscription now existing, yet we must remember that the language of the Bhilsa inscriptions is identical with that spoken at Vidisa, the home of Mahinda's mother, and this dialect differs in too many essential points from the Pāli for us to regard it as its origin. On the whole, the editor discredits the supposition that Buddhism was introduced into Ceylon as a developed system by the Prince Mahinda and his sister Sanghamitta, and leans to the belief that it was imported by degrees and by distinct advances from the neighbouring coasts of the Deccan, with which the people of Ceylon had very early and constant intercourse, and that the language therefore of these districts will furnish us with the answer to the question he asks as to the cradle in which the Pāli language was nurtured. He enforces this argument by some striking observations which ought to decide the question. The followers of the Sthavira school predominated in Ceylon, and were regarded as alone orthodox. Now this school existed nowhere in the North of India or in India proper (as we learn from Hiouen Thsang), except at Gayâ in the neighbourhood of the Bodhi-tree, in the convent founded by a king of Ceylon, and in which Ceylonese priests always found entertainment, as we are told the Northern priests were entertained at Nâlanda. It was in this very convent that Buddhaghosha was resident, and from it he went directly to Ceylon, encouraged or instigated to do so doubtless by conversation with priests from that country. But again, the Sthavira school was located chiefly on the eastern shores of India, from the mouth of the Ganges southward through the dominion of the Kaliñga and in the country of the Drâviḍa; and further, on the west coast in those parts which stood in connection with Ceylon, in Bharukaccha and Surâshṭra, and probably in the Malaya kingdom and in Andhra. From this fact, viz., of the popularity of the Sthavira school in these districts, and its decided supremacy in Ceylon, Dr. Oldenberg argues that the language of the one locality must be allied with, if it does not represent in all particulars, that of the other. He then compares with the Pāli what we actually know of the language of the kingdoms of Kaliñga and Andhra from ancient inscriptions, and from these he again argues that the Pāli is much more likely to have had its home in districts to the south, rather than the north, of the Vindhya mountains. He refers expressly to the inscription of the mother of Sâtakaṇṇi, king of the Andhra, found at Nâsik, and to the important though as yet partially unintelligible rock-inscription of Aira Mâhameghavâhana, king of the Kaliñga, discovered at Khandagiri, in Orissa. "It will be found," he says, "that the differences between the dialect of these inscriptions and the Pāli are not greater than can readily be explained from casualties relating to the different manner in which the texts were handed down on both sides." Perhaps, also, the sculptures found in the Ganeśa Gumpha and the Râj Rânî caves at Khandagiri refer to the conquest of the Rakshasis of Ceylon by Vijaya, in which case there is further evidence of the early connection between the two countries.

We are so far, then, led to the conclusion that the Pāli redaction of the Buddhist Canon, although an ancient one, and traditionally preserved, probably in Magadha in the neighbourhood of the Bodhi-tree, was yet only one of many versions of the discourses and precepts of the great Master as they were at one time known throughout India, and that the Sanscrit versions known in Nepal were translations, not from these Pāli Scriptures alone, but from works carried beyond the reach of persecution by Buddhist refugees from all parts of India. The character of the Chinese translations of the Sacred Books establishes this conclusion. We must bear in mind the historical connection of these books with the originals brought from India. Supposing that the first books were brought from that country no earlier than the time of Ming Ti, about the middle of the first century, yet this is a date early enough to give them a distinctly primitive character. And for six hundred years following this date there continued to flow eastward a stream of Indian merchants and Indian missionaries, who brought their books with them from every part of the country, and therefore, as we argue, written in widely different idioms. Moreover, the character of the Chinese versions of the same book, that is, of books having the same title, proves beyond doubt that the originals from which the translations were made, although founded on one and the same traditional record, were reduced to writing in distinct dialects, and probably widely separated districts. Let us take, for example's sake, two of the versions of the Life of Buddha known in China, and commonly regarded as different translations of the same original, generally called the Lalita Vistara. There were, according to Julien, four versions of this work, although I have only met with the second and the third. Still these two afford good ground for comparison. The third, which is called *Ta-chwang-yan-king*, is identical in its divisions and general text with that made from the Thibetan by M. Foucaux, which is again confessedly the same as the Sanscrit version known to us through the pages of the "Bibliotheca Indica," and commonly received in Nepal as one of the Sacred Books. The second Chinese version, on the other hand, known as the *Phŭ-yaou-king*, or the "Sûtra of Universally Diffused Light" (Samanta Prabhâsa),[1] is found to differ from the Sanscrit in most material points. The general thread of the story is the same, and in some passages there is an identity of expression, but yet in others the narratives differ in essential points, and the details are evidently of a different traditional school. How is this to be explained? It appears to me that the reason is this: The translator of the *Phŭ-yaou-king* was an Indo-Scyth, or a White Hun, who lived at Tun-hwang, beyond the great wall of China; his name was Dharmaraksha, and he flourished just about the middle of the third century A.D. We read that he travelled through all the countries of the western world (*i.e.*, India and its neighbourhood), and understood the dialects and could read the books of thirty-six kingdoms. On his return from India, he brought with him an immense store of Buddhist and Brahman literature, written in the *Fan* language—that is, one of the languages referred to

[1] This is the Sanscrit restoration of the title; but it is by no means certain that the work is Sanscrit.

above; and bringing them to the imperial court of China, he took up his abode at Loyang, and there, for a period of forty-three years, devoted himself to the work of translation. He rendered in all 165 works into Chinese from various originals, and amongst these the Life of Buddha which is reported to be another version of the Lalita Vistara. The reason, then, of the wide differences between this work and the next version, which is in strict agreement with the Sanscrit, is this: That Dharmaraksha procured his MS. somewhere in the course of his travels, and that it was not written in Sanscrit, but some Prakrit dialect —one of the thirty-six dialects, in fact, which he is reported to have understood, and from this he rendered it into Chinese. Now what is true in this case is so in many others, and none more so than in the different versions of the Vinaya Piṭaka which we have in the Chinese Canon, and to which I now wish to call your attention.

I have observed in my Catalogue of the Buddhist Canon as known in China and Japan, p. 110, that we have in those countries copies of the Vinaya Piṭaka as received in the different schools of Buddhism, which are elsewhere unknown. First, we have the *Shi-song-liu*, or the Vinaya of the Sarvâstavâdins; then the *Mo-ho-seng-chi-liu, i.e.*, the Vinaya according to the Mahâsanghika school; next the *Sse-fen-liu*, or the Vinaya according to the Dharmaguptas; then the *Ni-sha-sa-po-wu-fen-liu, i.e.*, the Vinaya of the Mahisasikas; then the *Kan-pen-shwo-yih-tsai-yau-po-pi-ni-ye, i.e.*, the Vinaya of the Mûlasarvâstavâdins, and corresponding works related to these. It would be impossible to enter on a detailed examination of all these books, although I believe that such a scrutiny would go to establish the dialectical differences of the originals, which differences were to a great extent the cause of the schisms which occurred in the Buddhist Church, and so establish the existence of various Prakrit copies of the Canon. I shall therefore confine the few remarks I have to make to two copies of the Vinaya in the Chinese Tripiṭaka, viz., that made from the writings of the Mahâsanghika school, and the other from the Mahisasika school. The Vinaya of the Mahisasika school—this school being a branch of the early sect known as the Sarvâstavâdins—is allied to the Mahâsthavira school, recognised as orthodox in Ceylon.

This copy of the Vinaya, therefore, is found to agree most closely with the Southern copy, as far as we yet know it through the edition being published of Dr. Oldenberg.

The Mahâsanghika school, on the other hand, was a school that split off from the Sthavira, or school of elders, and represents the teaching of the body of priests as differing from the leaders. These two schools, in fact, represent as nearly as possible the aristocratic and democratic elements found in almost all religious communities.

The Chinese version of the Mahisasikas was made by a priest called Buddhajiva, or it may be Buddhayasa, who lived in Cophene, or the Cabul district of India, towards the end of the fourth century A.D. The Mahâsanghika version was made by two priests, one a native of North India, viz., Kapilavastu, and called Buddhabhadra; the other a Chinese priest well known to us as Fă-hien. Buddhabhadra was a direct descendant of Amritodana, the uncle of Buddha Gotama, and was induced to visit China by a priest, *Tchi-yen*, who had been one of Fă-hien's companions.

The method of Buddha's teaching, as illustrated by these books, was this:—First surrounding himself with disciples who accepted the great principles of his system, he framed for their guidance certain directions as the occasion arose, and these directions became afterwards precedents for other cases of a similar kind. Thus we read at the beginning of the first section, or the Pârâjika division of the Mahisasika school—"Buddha was residing in the Savatthi country with five hundred great Bhikshus; from this country he proceeded to the town of Verañja, so called from the name of a Brahman whom King Prasenajita had placed there as governor. This nobleman, hearing that Buddha and his followers were residing outside the town in a wood sheltered by the trees—[for as yet there were no vihâras or convents built]—and understanding his character as the perfectly enlightened teacher of gods and men, the great discerner of all hearts, the preacher of the immaculate law, and that he in his travels had found his way there, was filled with joy, and exclaimed, 'I must go see this Buddha!' So with five hundred of his immediate friends, surrounded thus by them, he went to the place where Buddha was, to see him. And when he beheld him at a distance seated in the grove under a tree, his body and members perfectly in repose, and surrounded by a halo of glory, he was filled with joy; and alighting from his chariot, he advanced towards the sage, and after saluting him respectfully, stood on one side. On this Buddha preached in his hearing the excellent law, showing its profit and its blessedness; on hearing which Verañja was filled with joy and addressed Buddha as follows:—'I pray my Lord Buddha and his followers to receive at my hands daily charity during[1] the three months of rest' (Wass). To whom Buddha replied, 'My followers are numerous, and you are of a different belief, of different views, of different persuasion (joy), of a different mode of worship.' To which Verañja answered, 'Although this be so, yet I pray you comply with my request.' And having repeated his invitation three times, Buddha consented; and then rising from his seat and circumambulating Buddha with his right hand towards him, he departed and returned home to make the necessary preparations for three months' entertainment. Now Mâra Pisuna at this time reflected with himself thus: 'This Brahman has invited Buddha and his followers to spend the three months of rest at his abode and receive his entertainment. I must cause him to forget his engagement by my bewitchments.' Having thought thus, he forthwith came, and by his delusive power caused him to forget his invitation. In consequence, the Brahman, having gone into his inner apartments to indulge in every kind of pleasure, gave orders to the gate-keepers thus: 'I am going to enjoy myself for three months within doors; whatever business occurs, good or bad, let me not be troubled;' and so he forgot all about his invitation to Buddha and his followers. Now because this was an heretical country, there were no places of rest or preaching halls in any of the towns or villages. But to the north of the city there was a hill covered with trees and free from impurities; thither Buddha and his followers went to pass the three months of rest. And now came a season of much distress; for though they regularly begged through the streets of the city, but little was given to them, and the whole community was without food.

[1] Or it may perhaps be, *after* the three months.

At this time there was a certain horse-dealer of the *Pa-li* country who was travelling with 500 horses, and, on account of the extreme summer heat, he looked round for a place of shelter, and seeing that the country round Verañja was cool and rich in grass, he halted there and fed his horses. At this time the Bhikshus, coming to the place where the horse merchant was encamped, silently stood before him and begged for alms. Then the merchant, from a principle of faith in Buddha, and filled with pity because the Bhikshus were unable to get food, spoke thus: 'I have some grain which I give to the horses; if you are able to eat this, I can give you half a pint each for the purpose of strengthening you along the way.' Whereupon the Bhikshus thought thus: 'Buddha has given us no permission to eat such food as this.' Whereupon they came to their master and told him the circumstance. On this Buddha summoning the Samgha to a council, addressed them on the happiness of contentment and submission, and then added: 'From this time forward I permit you to eat food fit to be given to horses.' Then Ânanda, taking Buddha's share of grain, the attendants making it into a cake, presented it to the world-honoured one. Then the Bhikshus, grinding theirs with a pestle, ate it (at the usual time)."

From this opening incident of the Pârâjika section we observe the early practice of travelling from place to place adopted by Buddha. He seems to have been accompanied by his chief disciples, and have trusted to the charity of the people for his support. We see that his fame was spread wherever he went, and that even unbelievers were aware of his character. This story of Verañja offering Buddha and his followers hospitality during the three summer months exhibits the tolerance which at that time existed between the different sects. There is here no sign of hatred or malevolence between Brahman and Shaman, which afterwards marked the history of Buddhist development. Nor did Buddha decline the hospitality of an unbeliever. Again, we observe the decidedly Semitic idea of Satan bewitching and possessing the mind of men with a view to accomplish his end—that is, of resisting the advance of Buddha's kingdom—for of this we are repeatedly reminded through the history of the Teacher, that he and Mâra were ever opposed, their aims and objects being different. We also see the method in which the rules that afterwards became the code of the Buddhist Church were first framed. They arose from different circumstances affecting the immediate necessity of the Church. In this case, *e.g.*, the disciples were in distress for food; the authorised provision was that usually prepared in households, viz., rice and milk or rice and honey. But being unable to obtain this, the rule was relaxed, and oaten cake was allowed to be used for food. And throughout the Vibhangha section of the Vinaya this method is adopted; the immediate circumstance being reported to Buddha, he convenes an assembly of priests, and the rule is framed by his permission and sanction, which afterwards remains in force as a part of their daily discipline.

The next incident of the section before us is one that illustrates the claim made by the chief of Buddha's followers to miraculous powers. "At this time the worshipful Mugalan[1] (one of the *aggasāvakas*, or chief disciples, two in number), dwelling in retirement, thought thus with himself: 'It is difficult to beg food in this country, for none is given; now then I will use my spiritual power and pass at once to the Uttara-kuru (the Northern continent), and partake of the naturally-produced rice that grows there.' Having thought thus, he forthwith arose and came to the place where Buddha was, and bowing at his feet, he stood on one side and addressed him thus: 'World-honoured! I have had the following thought: This country is hard to beg food in; I will use my spiritual power and go to the Northern continent, and there partake of some of the rice that grows of itself.' To whom Buddha replied, 'You indeed have this power, but what will the other priests do?' To whom he answered, 'I will carry them also by my spiritual power to the same place.' To which Buddha answered, 'Nay! nay! although you have this power, and can use it when the occasion arises, yet you can by no means extend it to others, nor by your own action affect the rest of the priests.' Mugalan having been thus instructed, was silent, and remained on the spot."

Here we see again the method of teaching common in the early Buddhist community. Whatever this power claimed by Mugalan might have been, he was checked in exerting it by

[1] I write the name of Maudgalyâyana thus, because the Chinese symbols are *Mu-lin*.

the express command of the Master, and its limits were defined. He was, moreover, reproved for the selfish aim he had in view, and was forbidden to use his supernatural energy for such a purpose as mere self-gratification.

The next incident throws light on the origin of the code of rules, which gradually extended itself to the most minute cases of conscience. "At this time the worshippful Sâriputra (the other of Buddha's chief supporters, *aggasāvakas*), whilst dwelling in retirement, thought thus with himself, 'Which of the moral systems of all the ancient Buddhas did not last long, and which of these systems did endure?' Then rising from his seat, he forthwith came to the place where Buddha was, and bowing at his feet, again arose and stood on one side. He then addressed Buddha and said, 'I have just been thinking which of the moral systems of the ancient Buddhas did not, and which of them did endure.' At this time the world-honoured one much commended Sâriputra and said, 'Well spoken! well spoken! Your thoughts are good and your words are good, Sâriputra! Vipasyin Buddha, Sikhi Buddha, Visvabhû Buddha, the systems of these teachers did not endure long. But the systems of Krakuchanda Buddha, of Kanakamuni Buddha, and of Kâśyapa Buddha did last long.' Sâriputra then inquired, 'By what reason, world-honoured one, was this so, that the systems of three Buddhas endured not, and those of three Buddhas did endure?' Then Buddha addressed Sâriputra, and said, 'The three Buddhas first named did not extensively declare their law for the sake of their followers, and did not *bind*[1] their rules as a code,—did not deliver the Pratimoksha; and so after their Nirvâna, their disciples, through lack of discipline, were scattered and demoralised; just as when a vessel is filled with loose flowers, as they are carried thus along the streets of a town, a mighty wind arises and scatters them in every direction because they are not bound together by bands; so it is, Sâriputra, the doctrines of the three before-named Buddhas did not last, because they delivered no clearly expressed law, they did not connect their rules into a code, they did not frame a system like the Pratimoksha. But with reference to the

1 Does this provide us with a probable derivation of *Patimokkam*, as Childers suggests, *sub voc.* (*vid. infra*)?

other three, their systems *did* endure because they attended to these things. With respect to Visvabhû,[1] Buddha indeed, when he entered the grove called *the awful*—for in this grove those who had not yet given up the world were filled with fear and awe at the presence of the teacher—then he sat pondering in his mind a system for the direction of his followers, what they ought to reflect upon and what not, what to do and leave undone, what to practise and what to rely upon. Thinking thus, he yet spake nothing; nevertheless, his disciples, divining his thoughts, were enabled to cast off all remnants of personal thought and to become Rahats. But in the case of Kanakamuni Buddha and Kâśyapa Buddha, these two delivered at large their doctrines for the sake of their followers, so that there could be no forgetfulness on their part; and the law they thus announced comprised Sûtras, Geyas, Viyâkaranas, Gâthâs, Udânas, Nidânas, Itiyuktas, Jâtakas, Vaipulya, Abhutadharma, Avadânas, Upadesas; and they, moreover, announced the system of the Pratimoksha, so that after their Nirvâna their disciples were not scattered or demoralised, just as a wreath of flowers securely bound together when carried through the streets cannot be scattered by the winds. And why? Because they are tied together by a string. It was for these reasons that the code of rules established by these Buddhas endured for a long time.' Sâriputra again addressed the Buddha, and said, 'Oh, world-honoured one! if this is the reason of their non-endurance, would that thou also wouldest enumerate a well-considered (expanded) system of doctrine, and also deliver a code of rules well secured as with a string, called Pratimoksha, for this is a favourable opportunity for doing so.' Then Buddha replied, 'Nay, Sâriputra, I know my own time. My congregation of followers is not yet prepared to receive such an ample code of laws, but in time they will be prepared.'"

I shall now direct you to the next paragraph in the Vinaya, and afterwards proceed to a consideration of the two councils.

At this time, the narrative proceeds, after the three months' rest had expired, the world-honoured one addressed Ananda and said, "Let us go together, Ânanda, to the dwelling of Verañja."

[1] This seems to be a mistake for *Krakuchanda* Buddha.

Having received this order, Ânanda, arranging his clothes in the orthodox manner, followed Buddha and arrived at the door (of Verañja's house). At this time the Brahman was dwelling at the top of the tower of his abode, indulging himself in the practice of the five worldly pleasures. Seeing the world-honoured one at a distance coming towards his house, immediately recollecting his promise, he came downstairs in haste, and at once dusting and arranging a seat, he fell down on the ground before Buddha and did him homage, whilst he thus penitently expressed himself: "I am indeed a foolish and wicked man, to have asked my lord to an entertainment, and now, at the end of the season of rest, to have made no preparations. Oh, that my lord would accept my regrets and repentance!" Buddha replied, "You are indeed a foolish and ignorant man to have asked me and my followers to an entertainment, and yet at last to have provided nothing. You ought rightly to be sorry and to repent of such conduct; but yet both I and my followers will accept your expression of regret. Moreover (Buddha added), according to my sacred law, those who repent of their sins should show it by increased attention to their religious duties." Then the Brahman replied and said, "I pray you then, my lord, to dwell with me one month, that I may bestow on you and your followers the charity of my offerings." But Buddha declined to accept this offer, adding, "You, O Brahman, are of a different faith and a different persuasion!" And although he pressed his request three times, still it was refused. At length the Brahman replied, "At least, my lord, condescend to accept my charitable offerings for one day, to-morrow." This offer Buddha accepted, signifying his acquiescence by silence. On this the Brahman began to make all preparations, providing food, arranging seats; whereupon, on the morrow early, Buddha and his followers arrived, on which the Brahman with his own hand handed to them their food, and afterwards water for washing themselves, and finally offered to them different-sized slippers as presents given after the time of rest. On this the Bhikshus appealed to Buddha, saying that as yet they had no authority for receiving such gifts. On which the Master, speaking to them on the blessedness of contentment, and having commended them for attending to his rules, added, "For the sake of Verañja, O Bhikshus! from this time forth I permit you to receive presents at the time of the conclusion of Wass."

From the above extracts we may gather an idea of the character of Buddha's teaching. I will now ask you to consider further the two Councils.

INTRODUCTORY.

Although the division of Buddhism into schools, viz., the Northern and Southern, has been generally accepted since the time of the publication of Eugène Burnouf's *Introduction*, yet, as I have observed in the previous section, we must hesitate before accepting the statement that the former school depends entirely upon *Sanscrit* versions of the Buddhist Scriptures, as the latter does upon *Pāli*.

Undoubtedly the Nepalese Buddhist Books are in Sanscrit, but the greater part of the Chinese Scriptures are translated from various Indian Prakrits, and from these Chinese versions are derived, to a large extent, the Thibetan and Mongolian sacred books.

Being translated into Chinese, these books bear the impress of their origin, principally in the form of the proper names, which are rendered phonetically into that language.

Thus, for the Sanscrit *Srâvastî*, the early Chinese Buddhist books have the Prakrit form *Savatthi;* for *stūpa* we find *ṭap*, and so on, proving that the translations were made either from MSS. written in some non-Sanscrit dialect, or else rendered into Chinese by word of mouth from foreign priests who did not speak Sanscrit.

We should expect, then, to find many of the books of the Southern Canon in China; translated, not necessarily from Pāli, but from dialects more or less resembling the Pāli, into the language of that country. And this is so. For instance, I find that the first Sutta in the Chinese version of the Samyutta-nikāya is the same as the Kasíbháradvaja Sutta of the Sutta Nipāta, which last, however, is a portion of the Khuddaka Nikāya in the South and not of the Samyutta Nikāya.

Without reprinting the English version of this Sutta (which

forms part of the translation of the Sutta Nipáta by Sir M. Coomára Swámy, p. 20 *seq.*), I will produce my own version from the Chinese, and leave the comparison to those who are interested in the study and possess the little book above named.[1]

The T'sa-ho-hom-king (*Samyuktâgama Sutta*).

SUTTA I.

I have heard thus:—On a certain occasion Buddha was residing in the Ku-sa (Kosàla) country, accompanied by many Bhikshus. Thus accompanied, he was journeying through a certain district,[2] and at length rested in the village called Ekanāla,[3] between some cedar trees. At this time an agriculturist (*kasī*) of the Brahman caste, whose name was Po-lu (*Bhára*), had assembled outside the village of Ekanāla some 500 ploughmen, all of them about to receive their morning food. At this time Buddha reflected thus—The day dawn is at hand; I will now go and pass in front of the dwellings in Ekanāla (for the purpose of obtaining food). At this time, then, these ploughmen were assembled to take their meal. Buddha arriving at the place where they were thus assembled, the agriculturist Bhára seeing Buddha thus approaching, when he had arrived addressed him as follows:—

"I with my own hand plough and sow, and when I have thus ploughed and sown, I eat the fruits of my work; you also, Gotamâcharya, should plough and should sow, and having ploughed and sown, you also might eat."

Buddha, replying to the agriculturist (*kasī*), said, "I also plough and sow, and having ploughed and sown, I eat."

The agriculturist answered Buddha thus, "Although Buddha says, 'I plough and sow, and having ploughed and sown, I eat,' yet, sir, I see no instruments of agriculture (in your possession), neither ox, nor yoke, nor goad, nor ploughshare."

And so again the agriculturist (Bhára) addressed (Buddha),

[1] The Chinese version dates, at any rate, earlier than the *Wu* dynasty, for it appears in a catalogue of Buddhist books prepared during that period, which lasted from A.D. 222 to A.D. 264.

[2] Called, "the district of bamboos," or, perhaps, "the Nāla district."

[3] Literally, "the one bamboo."

"I see not your instruments for sowing, and yet you say you sow; cause me to know of your sowing."

Buddha replied, "Faith is the seed, discipline is the rain, wisdom is my ox, modesty is my plough, mind is the string, thought is the golden (shear). My body guarded, my speech guarded, these are the ridges; unceasing practice of entire truth and self-government, this is the end (aim);[1] perseverance without any relaxation is the yoke; going on without stopping is the rest[2] (I enjoy); thus going on and not returning, I go to a place where there is no more sorrow. Thus it is, having sown, from thus sowing I enjoy the nectar (of life); by thus sowing I obtain final release from all sorrow."

Then Bhára the agriculturist, filling a vessel full of food, standing in front of Buddha, said, "Of a truth, O Buddha! thou art able to till the ground; verily, O Buddha! thou art a great tiller! Accept then, I pray, my food."

Then Buddha, compassionating him, replied thus:—"He who repeats the scriptures may not on that account accept food. This is the law for those disciples possessed of self-knowledge. Whenever Buddha has been thus asked (to preach), this has ever been the rule. By adding to the cause of religion, the only aim being to release the hearers from the bands of doubt, this is the food and drink I enjoy; this is the sacrifice I offer for the good and religious merit of others."

Then the Brahman replied, "To whom then shall I give this food?"

Buddha answered, "There is none in the world nor among the gods, whether Mâra, or Brahman, or Shaman, not one who, taking this food, would be able to derive from it nourishment (digest it). Only a Buddha or one who has obtained supreme wisdom can digest such food. Taking it, therefore, go to some place where there is water without insects, and put it on the surface, or seek out a void space where there is no grass, and bury it there." Then the Brahman having received these instructions, went to a spot where there was water without insects, and placed the food in it. Then when the food was thus placed,

[1] Perhaps it might be rendered "the furrows."

[2] This appears to be an intentional antithesis.

there came forth smoke and fiery bubbles, whilst a sound resembling the noise "*chhuy theĕ*"[1] proceeded from it. Just as a sheet of red iron (copper) which has been a whole day heated in the fire when placed in water hisses and causes fiery bubbles, and produces a similar sound (to that above named), so did this food when thus placed by the Brahman [as before].

Then the Brahman, terrified, his hair erect, prostrated himself at the feet of Buddha, and said, "May I be received by Buddha as a Shaman. I put away from me all evil, and take on me the religious rules and the practice of a religious life, according to Buddha's teaching." Buddha replied, "By leading a pure life, from this you may obtain supreme wisdom."

Then the Brahman was admitted by Buddha as a professed disciple, and took upon him the rules of a religious life, and in the end, walking in the law of Buddha, obtained the condition of perfect freedom (no impediment).

Thus it was said by Buddha."

It will be seen by comparing the above translation with that from the Sutta Nipáta, that the two agree so far as to render it likely that they were both translations from one original document, or both derived from a common source (tradition). The Chinese may be somewhat corrupt, but yet the identity can scarcely be denied.

It may be well, perhaps, as a further test, to add some brief abstracts of one or two Suttas which follow the above in the Samyuktâgama, as we know it in China. The Suttas are in themselves interesting as expositions of Buddhist doctrine, and will therefore repay the trouble of translation and perusal.

SUTTA 2.

I have heard thus :—On one occasion Buddha was dwelling in the garden of Jeta the friend of orphans, in the country of She-wei (Srâvastî). At this time a Brahman called *Sing-wen* (Birth-hearing[2]) came to the place where Buddha was for the purpose of asking him a question. Having come and occupied a place, he sat down. Having sat down, he then addressed Buddha as follows :—

[1] The Pāli gives "*chit, chit.*"

[2] Or *birth-renown.*

"I have heard it reported that Buddha says, 'Charity ought to be bestowed on me alone, and not on strangers. The merit of bestowing charity on me is great, but when bestowed on strangers it is not great. Charity should be shown to my disciples only; the merit of such charity is great; but when bestowed on strangers (followers of others) the merit is not great.' Those persons who say thus, that your doctrine is that charity ought to be given to you and your disciples only, do they in so saying slander (the doctrine of) Buddha or not? Is this the principle of Buddha's teaching? Are these Buddha's words or not? Is this according to the Dharma or not? or is it a matter of indifference?"

Buddha replied thus to the Brahman:—"If people say that my doctrine is this, that charity should be given to me only and not to strangers, to my disciples only and not to others; that the merit of so doing to me and my disciples is great, but not so in the other case, &c., such reports are not true, not according to my teaching, not according to the Dharma, for in truth I say no such thing. Such doctrine as this would overthrow the principle of charity and merit in the case of creatures not yet brought within the reach of my doctrine. But, in fact, my teaching is this, that the slightest act of charity, even in the lowest class of persons, such as saving the life of an insect from a principle of pity, that this act has such merit as to cause the performer of it consequent benefit. And so in all cases, whatever the character of the person and whatever his position, whether black or white, red or yellow, even down to the very peacock, ox, or dove, that all these are benefited by acts of charity however bestowed, and according to their actions they must rise higher or fall lower in the scale of life. It is from these acts men rise and are born in heaven. It is from these actions also they sink and are born in the 'three evil ways.'[1] In this way, by their conduct in all conditions of being, creatures cause their own advantage or subsequent loss.

"The Brahman Sing-wen, hearing these words, rose from his seat, prostrated himself at the feet of Buddha, and from that

[1] *I.e.*, as a beast, a demon, or in hell.

time sought in him his refuge, and took upon him the precepts (*i.e.*, became a disciple).

"Buddha so declared."

SUTTA 3.

I have heard thus:—Buddha was at one time residing in the garden of Jeta, the friend of the orphans, at Śrâvasti. Whilst there, an aged Brahman (Thee-ho-ché) came to the place where Buddha was, and having exchanged salutations, he stood on one side and sat down. Having seated himself, he questioned Buddha thus:—

"To what resemblance may we liken the wicked man?"

Buddha replied, "We may liken the wicked man (in his course) to (that of) the moon."

Again he asked Buddha, "And if one wished to distinguish the good man from others, to what might we compare him?"

(To whom he replied), "The good man may also be likened to the moon."

Again he asked Buddha, "In what way does the unwise man resemble the moon?"

(Buddha answered), "Just as the moon on the 29th day of the month diminishes in brightness, loses its colour, is deprived of its shape, becomes lost and perishes, and after midnight is no more seen, so is it with the foolish and ignorant man. He has listened to the Scriptures explained by the wise; he has been taught the precepts; but though he has acquired knowledge and gained an acquaintance with wisdom and truth, he has not walked accordingly; he has not brought his heart to obey; on the contrary, he has let go his knowledge, neglected his conduct, disregarded his duty, so his faith has perished; his uprightness has perished; his attention to instruction has perished; his acts of charity have perished; his wisdom has perished; and at midnight he disappears, and is gone for ever. So it is, O Brahman! in one moment the wicked man entirely disappears, and is for ever lost as the moon on the 29th day. The wise man, again, may be compared to the moon on the 15th day of the month, increasing in brightness, completing its shape, becoming fuller and more perfect. At a certain moment it becomes perfectly round, and so remains for the time; thus also is it with the wise man; he shapes his life according to the words of his instructors; acquires true faith; adds to faith obedience; regulates his thoughts, keeps fast to the precepts, and so increases his faith; adds to his duty; adds to his attention to instruction; adds to his charity; adds to his wisdom; adds to his high endeavours; and so at midnight (as it were) he is full and complete. At the appointed time, his wisdom, his conduct, his pure life, his perfect obedience become thus rounded like the moon on the 15th day, and he shines out perfect and full for men to behold. And as the moon when it is full exceeds in glory and eclipses the light of all the lesser stars, so does the wise man shine out in the midst of his fellow-men. His wisdom, like the rain that waters the earth, is a blessing to those around him, causing increase and happiness, and finally (by his example and conduct) he brings many others to the happiness of a birth in heaven.

"The Brahman having heard these words, bowed low at the feet of Buddha, and took refuge in the doctrine.

"So Buddha declared."

Without continuing these translations, perhaps enough has been written for the purpose of comparison. We may, however, remark that there is a peculiarity in all the Northern Sûtras not known in the South. Buddha in the former works is never addressed as *Gotama*, whereas in the latter this is his common name. Whenever this title is used in the Northern books, it is put in the mouth of unbelievers, and is supposed to be employed in contempt. Thus, in the fifth Sûtra of the Samyuktâgama, a Brahman unbeliever called *Wou-sin-chung* (No-faith-degree) goes to the place where Buddha is dwelling for the purpose of refuting his doctrine. Before going, he reflects thus, "This Gotama Shaman is dwelling in the bamboo grove near Râjagriha; I will now go to the place where this Gotama Shaman is, and contradict him to his face," &c. But on his conversion the Brahman falls at the feet not of *Gotama*, but of Buddha (*the Enlightened*), and becomes a disciple. I have observed very few exceptions to this rule in the Northern books, and so far it may be useful as a slight guide in the examination of the origin of the division between the two schools.

But undoubtedly the most interesting and useful document for comparison is one common to both North and South, and contained in the Vinaya Piṭaka in either case. I mean the accounts given us of the two Buddhist Councils, the one supposed to have been held at Râjagriha, the second 100 years afterwards at Vesâlî.

We may state, although it is already well known, that in the Vinaya Piṭaka we find mention made only of two Councils, the two above named. But in the Buddhist Church (North or South) there are two others mentioned, viz., the one at Pataliputra under Aśoka dharma, which is the third according to Southern accounts, but is not recognised in the North; and the fourth, held in Kashmir under the great king Kanishka; this is ignored in the South, but accepted in Northern accounts. There is no need to enter into explanations regarding these last two Councils; they are neither of them named in the Vinaya, and therefore are not within the field of the present inquiry.

It will be necessary before considering the Councils to say a few words about the schools into which Buddhism separated during the first century or so of its existence.

It is satisfactory to find that there is an agreement both in the Northern and Southern accounts respecting this matter. "Among the local traditions of the Mahâvihâra in Ceylon there has been preserved an account of the eighteen sects which arose during the course of the second century after Buddha's death." So says Dr. Oldenberg.[1] In agreement with this there is a general consensus in the North that the old Buddhist Church split into eighteen sects about the time of the first Aśoka.

In the account given by *I-tsing*,[2] a priest of the Tang dynasty, in the introduction to his work *Nan-hae-khi-kwei-ch'ouen*, it is stated: "The origin of the different schools is not the same; the records of the western countries, however, only embrace four chief ones—1. The Arya mahâsañghika nikāya, which in Chinese is the same as the school of the Great Congregation (*Ta chung pou*); from this proceeded seven minor schools. In this school the three Piṭakas each contain 100,000 verses, making altogether 300,000 verses.

[1] Vinaya Piṭakaṃ, Introd. xli., Oldenberg.
[2] A brief Life of I-tsing will be found at the end of the last Lecture.

In Chinese these verses would perhaps fill 1000 kiouen (chapters). 2. The Aryasthavira nikāya, which in Chinese is the same as *Shing-chang-tso-pou* (*i.e.*, the Sacred School of the Elders); this divided itself into three minor sects. The number of verses in the Tripiṭaka in this school is the same as in the former. 3. Aryamûlasarvâstivâda nikāya, which in Chinese is rendered *Shing-kan-pen-shwo-yih-tsai-yeou-pou* (*i.e.*, the Sacred School which affirms that all things exist); from this school separated four minor sects. The number of verses in the Tripiṭaka accepted by this school is just about the same as in the former cases. 4. The Samriti nikāya,[1] which in Chinese is equivalent to *Shing-ching-liang-pou* (*i.e.*, the Sacred School of Correct Proportion) (measure); this school separated into four minor sects. The Tripiṭaka adopted by these contains 200,000 gâthas, the Vinaya containing 30,000 of these verses. This is what is generally accepted respecting the eighteen sects in India. With reference to the fifth school[2] sometimes named, I heard nothing of this in India."

The same author then proceeds to say that the various offshoots of these schools had different names and practices, but these could not be dwelt upon; suffice it to know that throughout the five Indies and in the southern maritime provinces, the "four Nikāya bodies" were always spoken of, and each treated with more or less respect according to the locality. In Magadha, the Sarvâstavâdins were much honoured, but in the Mahratta country not so much, but there the Sammatiyas were particularly honoured. In North India they were all Sarvâstavâdins; occasionally, however, one meets with members of the Mahâsañghikas. In the south, the Mahasthavira school is universally honoured. In Eastern India, in different countries each of the four schools has its adherents. In Ceylon, all are members of the Mahâsthavira school, and the Mahâsañghikas are driven away. All the maritime provinces of the Southern Sea, including ten different countries, honour alike the Sarvâstavâdins and the Sammatiyas.

[1] *San-mih-lih-ti-ni-kia-ye.* This reading differs from that generally found, viz., *san-mi-ti-pou*, *i.e.*, *Sanmitîyas*, or, as it ought to be rendered, *Sammatîyas*. *Vide* Jul. ii. 234, n.

[2] Is this the same as the *Khuddakanikāya*?

From the above remarks of the priest *I-tsing* it will be observed that the Tripiṭaka, as known in Ceylon, belongs to the Mahâsthavira school, and so his record is in perfect agreement with local tradition in that country. "According to the traditions of the Sinhalese, one of the schools possessed a claim to be considered as orthodox, on account of its having held fast to the original tradition of the Theras (*Mûlathera-vâda*); of course, the Sinhalese Church considers itself as belonging to this party."[1]

And if the conclusions of the same writer (Dr. Oldenberg) be correct, that "the Pāli writings of Ceylon belonging to this school embody the Vinaya in its original form," we have here some foothold for examination and comparison.

Let us then compare the account of the first Council held at Râjagriha, or more correctly supposed to have been held in the Satapanni cave near Râjagriha, as it is given in the closing chapter of the Cullavagga, in the Pāli, with the history of the same council as it is known in the North. I will take first of all the account found in the Dharmagupta version of the Vinaya Piṭaka. This school is an offshoot of the Sarvâstavâdins, who, in their turn, divided from the school of the Aryasthaviras, the dominant one in Ceylon.[2] We should, therefore, expect to find a marked agreement between the two accounts; and as the Dharmaguptas prevail mostly in the North, and their writings are generally accepted in China, the comparison will be an interesting one.

THE COUNCIL OF THE FIVE HUNDRED.

Translated from the 54th Book of the Vinaya Piṭaka known as Sse-fen-liu, i.e., Dharmaguptas.

At this time the world-honoured one (Lokanâtha,[3] *i.e.*, Buddha) was residing in the city of Ku-si (Kusinagara) in the Malla garden between the Sâla trees (or in the Sâla grove). Having here died (attained Nirvāna), all the Malla-

[1] Oldenberg, *op. cit.* xli.

[2] Jul. ii. 311, n. I-tsing, *Nan häe*, fol. 8.

[3] Stas. Julien always renders this title of Buddha by *Lôkadjyêchtha*, but the true restoration is probably either *Lokanâtha* or *Lokanâyako*.

putras having washed the body (*śarîra*) of Buddha, had wrapped it in clean linen, and then swathed it in five hundred folds of fine hair-cloth (like silk, *t'heë*). Then having made an iron coffin, and filled it with perfumed oil, they placed the body (thus prepared) in the middle of it, whilst over it they placed a canopy for protection. Again having constructed a wooden bier, they placed the coffin upon it, and below this they collected a heap of every kind of scented wood. Then at a given signal, the chief of the Mallaputras, taking a flaming torch, attempted to set fire to the wood. But the Devas immediately extinguished the flames. Again the great Mallaputras, encircling the pyre, holding flaming torches, (attempted to) ignite it. Once more the Devas extinguished the flames. Then Anuruddha addressed the Mallaputras thus :—"Weary not yourselves in vain; it is the Devas who extinguish the fire which you kindle."

On this they inquired of Anuruddha saying, "Venerable priest! (*ta tih*, Mahâbhadanta), why do the Devas extinguish the flames?" Replying, he said, "Mahâkaśyapa is now residing between P'o-po (Pāvā) and the city of Ku-si (Kusinâra); he is proceeding along the road with his great disciples, five hundred in all, thinking thus, 'May I perhaps be able once more to behold the body of Buddha ere it is consumed.' The Devas, perfectly acquainted with the thoughts of Kâśyapa, have on this account extinguished the flames." The Mallaputras replying said, "Venerable sir! let us then wait awhile in agreement with the intention of the Devas in so doing."

At this time then the great Kâśyapa, being, as before stated, on the road with five hundred of his great disciples (Bhikshus, *i.e.*, mendicants), between the two countries of Pāvā and Kusinâra, there came along a stranger, a Nirgrantha-putra, holding in his hand a Mandāra flower (which had fallen from space at the time of the death of the world-honoured one). Kâśyapa seeing him thus coming, addressed him as follows: "Whence come you, O friend! and whither go you?" Replying, he said, "I come from the city of Ku-si (Kusinagara)." Again he inquired, "Did you know then our Lokáyako (world-honoured), or not?"[1] He answered, "I knew him." Again he

[1] The Pāli gives *Satthá* for the Ch. "world-honoured."

asked, "Is he then still living or not?" He answered, "He is no longer living; seven days ago he died (attained Nirvāna), and I am come straight from the place of his death with this flower in my hand."

At this time Kâśyapa hearing these tidings was grieved; whilst those Bhikshus who were not yet free from passion [1] in his company, hearing that the world-honoured one was dead, fell down prostrate on the earth as a tree whose roots have been severed falls. Moreover, these Bhikshus, not yet freed from human passion, with wild lamentations cried, "Too early has the illustrious (good) one passed away (attained Nirvāna by death); too soon have the light-giving eyes of the world been put out; who now shall determine for us the right meaning of the law?" And so there were some who rolled upon the earth as dying men or lay still as logs of wood. Thus it was these Bhikshus, not yet freed from human passion, lamented and cried with grievous accents, "The Holy One too soon has died and attained Nirvāna! Alas! why is this?"

At this time there was a certain Sâkyaputra called *Balanda* [2] dwelling with the others, who addressed the Bhikshus thus: "Venerable sirs! stop your wailing. Grieve not thus, nor lament. We are now free from that great Rabbin.[3] Whilst he dwelt in the world he had various rules for our conduct; this thing you may do, this you may not do; this thing is right, that is wrong. But now we are free from all this and independent. If we wish to do a thing, we may do it; if we don't wish to do it, we need not do it." Then the great Kâśyapa hearing these words was much displeased, and forthwith addressed the Bhikshus, saying, "Rise up quickly and take your robes and your begging-dishes. Even now, perhaps, there is time to behold the body of the world-honoured ere it be consumed." The Bhikshus hearing the words of Kâśyapa, at once and without delay took their robes and their alms-dishes. And so the great Kâśyapa, with his 500 followers, went on towards the city Kusinagara. Having arrived and passed through the

[1] Ch. *mi-li-yuh*; Pāli *avītarāgā*.

[2] Called *Subhadra* in the Southern version.

[3] Ch. *Lopi'en*. This may be a misprint for *Lo-han*, *i.e.*, *Rahan*, but this last symbol is differently written a few sentences down.

city, they crossed the river Hiraṇyavati (*Hi-lan-yo*), and came to the *Thien-kwan* (God-beholding) Temple, to the place where Ananda was residing, whom he (Kâśyapa) thus addressed: "I desire, ere the body of the world-honoured be burnt, to behold it once more." Ananda answered, "I also desire to behold the body (*śarîra*) of the world-honoured once again ere it be consumed, but the thing is difficult. For why? They have washed the body of the world-honoured and enwrapped it in new linen; moreover, it is swathed in five hundred folds of hair-cloth, and thus prepared it is placed in an iron coffin filled with perfumed oil, and being put on a wooden bier, it is placed over a fire of scented wood, ready and waiting to be burned. This is the difficulty."

Then the great Kâśyapa proceeded gradually to the spot (leading the way as he went) where the body of the world-honoured one was placed. Arriving there, lo! the coffin opened by itself, and the foot (or feet) of the world-honoured one appeared. Then the great Kâśyapa beholding that the characteristic wheel-works on the soles of the feet were soiled, as it were, with dirt, addressed Ananda thus: "The person of our Master was beautiful and comely beyond description, his body of a pleasant golden colour; who then has caused this pollution on the wheel-signs on the bottom of his foot (or feet)?" Ananda answering said, "A woman with a tender heart came in front of Buddha's person and worshipped him; her tears rolling down fell upon her hands as she held his feet, and thus the marks were left as you now see them."

The Great Kâśyapa, hearing these words, was displeased. But now he bowed down and worshipped the feet of the world-honoured, whilst the Bhikshus, Bhikshunis, Upasakas, Upasikâs, Devas, and the whole multitude joined in the act of adoration; after this the feet withdrew within the coffin, and were no more visible. Then the great Kâśyapa, filled with joy, passed round the pyre seven times, reciting a hymn as he went, and lo! the wood, self-enkindled, flamed underneath the coffin and consumed it. After the cremation of the body, the great Kâśyapa, on consideration, assembled the body of priests together and addressed them thus: "When I was just now on the road travelling hither, I overheard Balanda speaking to the other Bhikshus and saying, 'Reverend sirs! stop your wailing,'

&c. (as before). 'We therefore ought to assemble together and go over the Dharma Vinaya, and so prevent the heretics and others, moved by envy, from such remarks as these: "The Dharma Vinaya rules of Gotama are like smoke; whilst he was in the world all obeyed his religious rules, but now he is dead and gone, there are none to follow his precepts." Now, then, reverend sirs, let us select carefully such Bhikshus as are men of renown, filled with wisdom, and have arrived at the condition of Rahatship!'"[1]

Accordingly they selected 499 men, all of them Rahats, men of renown for their great wisdom. Then they said, "We should also include Ananda amongst our number." But the great Kâśyapa replied, "Ananda cannot be admitted among the selected assembly. For why? Because Ananda is still subject to the passions of lust, anger, and ignorance (*rāga* (or, *chanda*), *dosa*, *moha*);[2] subject to these, he cannot therefore be admitted into the selected assembly." Then the Bhikshus said, "This Ananda was the personal attendant of Buddha, always accompanying him, who received from the world-honoured direct instruction in the Dharma in answer to all doubts that occurred. Surely he ought to be one of us."

The Bhikshus then considered, "In what place ought we to assemble in order to recite the Dharma Vinaya? It should be in a place where there is no lack of necessary food and drink, and a sufficient supply of sleeping materials (beds)." Then they agreed that the only place where such accommodation could be found was at Râjagriha; and it was in that place, therefore, that they ought to assemble to recite the Dharma Vinaya.

Then the Great Kâśyapa said: "Ye venerable men, hear me! Bhikshus! ye are those selected by the Sañgha. If the congregation (Sañgha) is ready, let the congregation hear me with patience. Let the congregation now proceed to the city of Râjagriha, and assembled there, let them recite the Dharma Vinaya."

---

[1] Here the symbols for *Arhat* are *O-lo-han*; but in the former case, where I have used the word *Rabbin* or *Rabban*, the symbols are *Lo-pi'en*.

[2] This, as I understand the Pâli, "*Kiñ câpi sekho, abhabbo chandâ, dosâ mohâ, bhayâ agatim*," is opposed to the Southern version.

Thus he spoke, and having spoken thus, they forthwith proceeded to Vesâlî.

Now Ananda, it happened, was upon this road going to a retired (pure) place (for the purpose of meditation), and whilst so going he thought thus within himself: "I am like a new-born calf, the only one who has to drink milk, whilst these five hundred Rahats are like full-grown oxen accompanying me."

Thus these great Bhikshus went onwards to Vesâlî, where Ananda remained. Whilst he remained there all the Bhikshus, Bhikshunis, Upasakas, Upasikās, the king of the country, the great ministers, Shamans of every calling, and heretics also, came in a body to pay their respects[1] to him—a vast concourse of people. At this time there was a Vajjiputra, a Bhikshu, possessed of great spiritual power (power to work miracles), who by the divine sight he possessed was able to read another's heart. Gifted thus, he reflected with himself: "Ananda is now residing in Vesâlî, the Bhikshus, Bhikshunis, &c., have all gone to salute him, a vast multitude of people. I will now examine and see whether there are any remnants of evil desire or not cleaving to Ananda." Thus examining and weighing the case, he found that Ananda was still subject to the influences of evil desire. Again he reflected: "I ought now to cause him to acquire a heart free from any such evil desire." With this purpose, therefore, he forthwith repeated the following verse:—

"Pure, and dwelling apart beneath a tree,
The heart fixed in thought upon Nirvāna,
Sitting thus in contemplation unrelaxed,
The world inquires—'What does he thus?'"

At this time Ananda, hearing the words of the Vajjiputra Bhikshu, having acquired a mind free from worldly desire, immediately proceeded to a lonely place and exerted himself without intermission,[2] perfectly quiet, without any mental disturbance: in this way Ananda exhibited in himself a miraculous power (of concentrated effort). At length, dwelling thus in the open space, he spread out his sleeping-mat, and at even-

[1] The Ch. *wen-sun* corresponds with the Pāli *abhivādeti*, as in the phrase, *Bhagavantam abhivādetvā.—Mangala Sutta.*

[2] The same phrase is used in the Mahavamsa, p. 13, l. 1.

time walked to and fro in thought. The evening past, the first streaks of dawn came on; and now, his body wearied (and his mind worn out) with excessive thought, he said, "Now I am wearied and worn-out with thought; I will sit down a while." Having so reflected, he sat down forthwith; having sat down, a desire for sleep overcame him, but ere his head had reached its resting-place, in the very interval as he was lying down, lo! his mind obtained perfect release.[1] Thus, by a supernatural effort (miraculous power) Ananda obtained the condition of a Rahat; and having so attained to this dignity, he forthwith repeated this verse:—

> "Well known for my much speaking,
> Ever engaged in attending upon the honoured one,
> Now having snapped the bonds of birth and death,
> The child of Gotama desires to sleep."

At this time, the Bhikshus having gone from Vesâlî and arrived at the city of Râjagriha, spoke thus among themselves: "What is the first business to be attended to? Shall we first arrange the dwelling-place and the sleeping materials (beds), or shall we at once proceed to recite the Dharmavinaya?" They all said, "We ought first to arrange the dwelling-place and the beds for sleeping;" and they at once proceeded so to do. Then the great Kâśyapa having in this wise assembled the Bhikshus, (they elected) as the first president (Sthavira) To-hi-lo Kâśyapa (Tara Kâśyapa ?), as the second Po-p'o-na (Pavana ?), as the third the great Kâśyapa, as the fourth the venerable Chau-na (Channa ?).[2]

Then the great Kâśyapa, at the right opportunity, forthwith addressed the assembly: "Venerable sirs! let the congregation attend; if the congregation is ready, let it patiently listen. We are now assembled to recite the Dharmavinaya." Thus he spoke. At this time Ânanda rising from his seat, baring his right shoulder and bending his right knee to the ground, with closed hands addressed the great Kâśyapa thus: "I who am a relative, remember hearing Buddha speak thus, 'From this time

[1] Ch. *won-lau-kiai-tuh*, corresponding, as it appears, with the condition of a Rahat.—*Mahavamsa*, *ut sup.*

[2] This passage has the appearance of a late interpolation. There is nothing corresponding with it in the Pāli.

forth, for the sake of the body of Bhikshus (I desire you to) except (exclude) from my code some miscellaneous offences [1] which have hitherto been binding upon them.' "

Kâśyapa inquired of Ananda, "Did you ask the world-honoured one or not what these minor offences were?"

Ananda replied, "At the time I was so overcome with grief that it escaped me to ask the world-honoured one what these exceptions were."

Then all the Bhikshus replied, "We then ought to decide what offences are not included amongst those which were remitted. The four *Pārājika* rules were not included (but all others were excepted).[2] The thirteen *Sanghadisesa* rules (others said) were not included, but all others were excepted. Again, others said, besides the four Pārājika and the thirteen Sanghadisesa rules, the two *Aniyatá dhamma* rules were not included amongst the number; others again said, besides the above, the thirty *Nissagiyá* were not included in the number; others said, besides the above, the ninety [3] *Nissagiya pácittiyá* rules were not included in the number.

Mahâkâśyapa then addressed all the Bhikshus, and said, "Venerable ones! (*aryasmanto*, Ch. *Chang lau*) as the case stands at present, men may well say there is nothing certain,—there is no sure knowledge about these minor offences. From this time, therefore, henceforth we ought to make it a fixed rule: What Buddha in former times did not make binding we ought not to bind; what he made binding we ought not to loose. In all cases we should be guided by his decision." To this rule, therefore, they all agreed.

The great Kâśyapa then addressed Ananda and said, "Because you first introduced women into the community of (those who profess) the Dharma of Buddha, you thereby became guilty of an offence (dukkata), and now you are called upon to confess and repent."

Ananda replied, "Venerable sir! this was not my doing (or done on my account), but because Mahâprajâpatî bore such great affection to Buddha, having so carefully cherished him

[1] These, doubtless, are the *Khuddánukhuddakáni sikkhápadáni* of the Pāli text.
[2] That is, as it seems, all others except *the four*.
[3] The Pāli gives ninety-two (*dvenavutiṃ*).

after his mother's death. Venerable sir! although I can see in myself no sinful conduct in this particular, yet, in submission to the judgment which you, venerable sir! have formed, I confess and repent."

The great Kâśyapa again said, "You caused the world-honoured to ask you three times to attend him as his personal follower, and then you replied it could not be. By thus doing you incurred guilt (dukkata), and must now confess and repent of your sin."

Ananda answered Kâśyapa and said, "It was not on my own account, but on account of the difficulty of rightly discharging such a duty that I declined. In so doing I do not see that I committed sin; but in submission to the judgment which you, venerable sir! have formed, I now confess and repent."

Kâśyapa again said, "When you undertook to sew (mend) the Sanghātī garment[1] for Buddha, you roughly put your foot upon it as you mended it. In so doing you were guilty of an offence (dukkata), and you should now confess and repent of it."

Ananda replied, "Venerable Kâśyapa! it was through no irreverence on my part that I did so, but to prevent any man seizing the robe. I do not recognise in myself any guilt in so doing. Nevertheless, in submission to your judgment, venerable sir! I confess and repent."

Kâśyapa again spoke: "When the world-honoured one desired death (to attain Nirvāna), three times he addressed you on the subject; but you neglected to request the world-honoured one to remain in life (the world), if it were only one kalpa, or more than one kalpa, for the benefit of countless mortals, for the display of his love and pity to the world, in obtaining for men and Devas the happiness of rest; in this you committed an offence (dukkata), for which you ought after confession to repent."

Ananda answered and said, "Venerable Kâśyapa! it was not my fault indeed, but the devil got possession of my heart, and caused me not to ask Buddha to remain in the world. In this thing I am conscious of no sinful purpose of my own. Never-

[1] The Pāli gives "*rain garment*

theless, venerable sir! I submit to your judgment, and confess and repent."

Kâśyapa again said, "The world-honoured one, when in the world, asked you to give him some water to drink, and you gave it not. In this you were guilty of an offence (dukkata), and you ought now to confess and repent of it."

Ananda answered and said, "It was not on my own account that I refused; but just then five hundred travelling waggons (chariots) had passed through the water, so that it was muddy and foul, and I feared to grieve the world-honoured one by offering him such water to drink, and therefore I refused to give it to him."

Kâśyapa replied, "You ought in any case to have given it, since Buddha by his own spiritual power, or through the instrumentality of the Devas, was well able to make the water pure and sweet."

Ananda said, "In this conduct I cannot condemn myself of sin; yet in submission to your judgment, venerable sir! I confess and repent."

Kâśyapa said again, "You did not ask the world-honoured one what were the minor offences he wished to have erased from his code (*i.e.*, *Khuddânukhuddakâni sikkhâpadanîti*, referred to before), you have thereby incurred the guilt of a dukkata (offence), and you ought to confess and repent of it."

Ananda replied, "It was not my own wilfulness, but because I was overpowered with grief, and so lost all self-possession, that I neglected to ask the world-honoured one the character of these faults. I see not that I thereby contracted guilt; nevertheless, in submission to your judgment, venerable sir! I now confess and repent."

Kâśyapa said again, "Because you did not prevent the woman polluting the feet of Buddha you were guilty of a dukkata (offence), and you should now confess and repent of it."

Ananda replied, "A woman with a tender heart worshipping at Buddha's feet, her tears falling fast upon her hands, soiled the (sacred) feet as she held them to her. In this I am conscious of no crime; nevertheless, venerable sir! in submission to your judgment, I now confess and repent."

And now the great Kâśyapa once more exclaimed, "Venerable sirs! let the assembly listen; if this be a suitable time,[1] let the assembly patiently attend. Is it the will of the assembly that I now question Upâli respecting the Dhammavinaya?"

(The assembly replying) "It is,"[2] then Upâli forthwith spoke, "Venerable sirs! let the assembly listen; if this be a suitable time, let the assembly patiently attend. Let the assembly cause the Sthavira, the great Kâśyapa, to question me as to what is the case (respecting the Dhammavinaya)."

Then the great Kâśyapa forthwith asked, saying, "The first *Pārājika* rule, in what place had it its origin? and who was the first offender (on whose account the rule was enacted)?"

Upâli replied and said, "It was at Vesâli, on account of the offence of Sudinna Kalandaputra, who was the first to commit the sin."

"In what place did the second rule come to be framed, and on whose account?"

"It was at Râjagriha, on account of the sin of the mendicant Dhanaka, the potter's son."

Again he asked where and on whose account the third rule was framed?

In reply he said, "At Vesâli, on account of the sin of Vaggumudātiriya[3] Bhikshu."

Again he asked, "Where and on whose account the fourth Pārājika rule was framed?"

He replied, "At Vesâli, on account of the same."

Again he asked, "Where was the first *Samghadisesa* rule framed?"

He replied, "In the country of Śrâvasti, on account of the sin of Kaludayi."

And in this way he went through the whole of the Samghadisesa rules, as the first.

Again he asked, "Where and on whose account was the first *Aniyatá dhammá* enacted?"

He replied, "In the Śrâvasti country, on account of Kaludayi's sin." [The second the same.]

---

[1] Pāli, *Yadi saṃghassa pattakallaṃ*.

[2] This translation is doubtful; it may be rendered "So that he may reply, *It is so.*"

[3] Chinese *P'o-kin-ho-pien*.

Again he asked, "Where did the rules called *Nissaggiyá* take their origin?"

He replied, "In the country of Śrâvasti, on account of the sin of the Sambahula[1] Bhikshus."

And in this way he went through all these rules.

Again he asked, "Where and on whose account was the first *Páccittiya* rule enacted?"

He replied, "At Shih-chi (Sachi?), on account of the Sākya-putra *Shau-siang-lih* (*Lean-elephant-strength*)."

And thus he went through all the *Pacittiya* rules.

Again he asked as to the place where the Pratidesaniyá rules were first enacted.

In reply he said, "At Śrâvasti, on account of the sin of the Bhikshuni Utpalavarna." [And so in reference to the three other rules under this section.]

Again he asked as to the place where the first of the *Sekkhiyá-dhammá* rules were framed.

In reply he said, "At Śrâvasti, on account of the sin of the Sambahula priests."

In this way he went through the whole of the rules, and those also relating to the Bhikshunis as they are detailed in the Book of Rules (the Vinaya; probably the Vibhanga).

Again he asked, "Who first of all accepted the great commandments (*i.e.*, the five rules of the Upâsaka), what was the cause and the place?"

Replying, he said, "It was at Benares, and the persons were the five mendicants" (viz., the five who were first converted).

Again he asked, "What was the occasion of the first enactment (repetition) of the rules (*i.e.*, the ten rules of the Sâmanera), who were the persons and in what place?"

He replied, "At Râjagriha, on account of the mendicants of tender age."

Again he asked, "Where did the ordinance respecting the 'retreat during the rains,' take its rise?"

He replied, "At Śrâvasti, on account of the conduct of the body of mendicants" (sambahute bhikkhû).

---

[1] The Chinese is *Luh-kwan*, "six company," nearly corresponding to the Pāli in the text.

Again he asked, "Where did the ordinance of the Pavâraṇâ festival (Ch. *tsz' ts'z*) take its rise?"

He replied, "At Śrâvasti, on account of the body of priests."

Thus it was he went through the various questions relating to the Vinaya, even down to the different occasions on which the priests were assembled for adding other regulations to the existing ordinances, detailing, moreover, the place where the assembly was made, whether for matters relating to the Bhikshus or Bhikshunis; as, for example, after questioning him on the appointment of the laws (Sikkhapadas) binding on the community, he proceeded to ask respecting the assembly held for enacting certain minor rules (*kien-to, i.e., Khandhaka* rules) relating to this point. So also with reference to the Uposatho rules and the place where the minor regulations (Khandhakas) were enacted; so also with respect to the retreat during the rainy season, and the place where, &c.; also respecting the Pavâranâ festival, &c.; so also respecting the rules relating to "shoes and slippers," &c. (articles made of skins); also respecting the rules relating to mendicants, &c.; also relating to the Kaṭhina ceremonies, &c. Thus he went through the whole of the regulations and their minor divisions, adding, moreover, the "harmonising sections" (*tui po*; probably the *Parivāra-pātha*), until the whole of the Vinaya Piṭaka was settled.

And now the great Kâśyapa addressed the assembly of priests as follows:—"Venerable sirs! let the assembly listen; if this is a suitable occasion, let the assembly patiently attend whilst we question Ananda respecting the Dhammavinaya, that he may reply, 'It is so.'"[1] Ananda forthwith arose and said, Venerable sirs! let the assembly listen; if this is a suitable occasion, let the assembly patiently attend. Let the assembly now direct the great Kâśyapa to question me whilst I answer, 'It is so.'"

The great Kâśyapa forthwith questioned Ananda and said, "In what place was the Fan-tung[2] (Brahmajāla) Sûtra delivered? In what place was the 'adding one' spoken? in what place was the 'adding ten' spoken? (These two last Sûtras probably refer to the *Anguttara nikāya*, or Âgama.) In what place was the Sûtra relating to 'the perfection and destruction

[1] Ch. *Ju shi.* The usual phrase beginning the Suttas, "*Thus* have I heard."
[2] *Tung* for *Kong*.

of the world' spoken? In what place was the 'Seng-tchi-to' Sûtra spoken? (This may possibly be the *Sañgha-gâtha*, corresponding to the *Thera-gâtha* of the South.) In what place was the Mahānidâna Sûtra spoken? In what place was the Sûtra relating to 'questions asked by Śâkra-râja' spoken?"

To all these questions Ananda answered according to what is found in the Dīgha-nikaya. From his replies the long Sûtras were collected into the 'Long Collection' (Dīgha-nikāya). The middle-length Sûtras were collected into the Majjhima-nikāya. The "from one to ten" subjects, and from "ten to eleven," and so on, were collected into the 'add one' (Aṅguttara) collection. Whilst the miscellaneous treatises relating to the Bhikshus, Bhikshunis, Upâsakas, Upâsikās, the Devas, Śakra, Brahma, Māra, and so on, were collected into the mixed volume of Sûtras (Samyutta-nikāya).

So also he replied concerning the Jātaka Sûtra, the "good" Nidāna Sûtra, the Vaipulya Sûtras, the Adbhuta (dharma) Sûtras, the Avadâna Sûtras, the Upadesa Sûtras; the Ku-i ("meaning of sentences") Sûtra, the Dharmapada Sûtra, the *Po-lo-yen*[1] Sûtra, the "concourse of dangers" Sûtra, the verses of the Holy One (Muni gâtha), all these, composing the miscellaneous collection of Sûtras (Khuddaka-nikāya?) he spoke of; so also of others, in which difficulties and no difficulties in meaning were discussed, all these in their turns he spoke of, and so was collected the Abhidharma Piṭaka.

At this time the collection of the three baskets (Piṭakas) being finished, the venerable Purana hearing that the 500 Arhats had assembled in convocation at Râjagriha (to arrange) the Dharmavinaya, immediately set out with 500 of his own followers (Bhikshus) for Râjagriha. Having reached the place where the great Kâśyapa was, he spoke as follows:—

"I hear, great sir! that you have assembled with 500 Arhats to arrange the Dharmavinaya. I also wish to hear the list of these, that I may also concur with you in the selection."

Then the great Kâśyapa, on this request, again assembled the congregation of Bhikshus, and for the sake of this Bhikshu (*i.e.*, Purana) again questioned Upāli, and so forth, until the whole

---

[1] This may possibly be the *Parinivâna* Sûtra.

of the three Piṭakas had been discussed (as before detailed). Then he said, "Venerable Kâśyapa! all this is right, and I confirm what has been said, only excepting the eight things which Buddha allowed. Venerable sir! I, who am related to Buddha (or, my friends who are related to Buddha), heard from him and clearly remember that he allowed his followers to partake of such things as ripened of themselves, or were decaying (from ripeness), or were inwardly ripe, he allowed them to take such things themselves and eat them at the time of their rising in the morning, and from that time forth it has been usual to eat of various fruits, and that which 'can be gathered from water.' There should, then, be no exception made to this rule."

The venerable Kâśyapa in reply said, "It is true, as you say; the world-honoured one, during a scarcity of food among the people, when it was difficult to get food by begging, mercifully permitted the Bhikshus to eat things of this eightfold kind. But when the scarcity was over and a time of plenty returned, and there was abundance to eat and drink, then Buddha again withdrew his permission and forbade these things."

Then Purana answered, "Venerable Kâśyapa! the world-honoured one, who was possessed of all knowledge, ought not, having once bound his disciples by law, to loosen the law; nor having loosened, ought he again to have bound them."

Then Kâśyapa replied, "It was because the world-honoured one was possessed of all knowledge that he was permitted to bind and loose as he desired."

Purana replied, "We also (*i.e.*, my followers) make this our rule (binding): that which *Buddha* did not bind, *we* do not bind; that which *Buddha* bound, *we* also bind and dare not loose. The rules which Buddha enacted, these we must stand by and obey (learn)."

"(The assembly of the five hundred Rahats at Rájagriha, for the purpose of settling the Dhammavinaya, commonly called the Assembly of the Five Hundred.)"

Comparing this translation with the Pāli text of the Cullavagga, we find several points of divergence,[1] but the two texts

[1] Oldenberg, Vinaya Piṭaka, vol. ii. p. 284.

are evidently either derived from a common source, or the one is a corrupt version of the other. It is more natural to suppose that both were reduced to a written form from a common tradition, at different periods, and in different places. This view would satisfy the requirements of the case, and is favoured by what we actually know about Buddhist books. It was with much difficulty that Fa-hien, in the fifth century of our era, could find written copies of the Vinaya in India. The substance of them was handed down by word of mouth. This fact alone is sufficient to account for differences, independent of the schools to which the texts belong.

Comparing the two more closely, we observe that the brief account of the cremation of Buddha's body is wanting in the Pāli, which opens with the words of Kâśyapa himself relating his encounter during his journey from Pawa with the Nirgrantha (or, as he is called in the Pāli, the "ājīvako") who had witnessed the death of Buddha. In the *Sarvâstavadin* version of the Vinaya the whole history of the cremation is given, with the division of the relics and the subsequent events relating to the erection of Stūpas over them. In the version before us there is but a bare allusion to these matters, whilst in the Pāli all reference to them is absent. Are we to suppose then that the Parinibbana Sutta, in which these particulars are found, was incorporated into the body of the Sarvâstavadin Vinaya at a late date, or that the particulars respecting the death of Buddha and the division of his relics formed a part of the original Vinaya, and were afterwards eliminated and formed into a separate work, viz., the "*Parinibbana Sutta*"? The last hypothesis, although it would account for the gradual disappearance of the introductory matter found in the Northern version of the Vinaya, would not be satisfactory in the face of the early redaction of the Pāli version, and the undoubted priority of the Sthavira school to the others. We must conclude, therefore, that the extraneous matter found in the Northern accounts of the council was incorporated with the Vinaya at the time of its redaction, whilst in the South it remained in the form we there find it, viz., as a separate and a primitive Sutta.

The history of the woman who wept at Buddha's feet is

curious, and as it is referred to in the Pāli, it cannot be a late interpolation. The weeping *at his feet* indeed is not named in the Pāli, but the statement respecting the tears soiling his person (sarîra), evidently alludes to the circumstance named in the Chinese text.[1]

The curious title given to Buddha, "Lo-pi'en," which can only be restored to "Rabbin" or "Rabbân" (unless indeed the symbol "pi'en" be a misprint for "*han*," which is most unlikely, as the compound *O-lo-han* for Rahat occurs only a few lines down), would seem to point to a Syriac origin,[2] and if so, would strengthen the supposition that there was intercourse between India and Syria at an early date, unless we accept the statement of a recent writer that *Rab* or *Rabu* is a Babylonian title meaning "great."[3] At any rate, this would simplify the matter, as the intercourse between India, especially North India, and the district bordering on Babylonia is undoubted, and has left its impress on Buddhist architecture and ornament still visible.

We have only space to refer to one other peculiarity in the record here translated, and that is, the allusion to the division of the Buddhist Scriptures into *angâni* or classes. This division, it has been recently shown,[4] is by no means a modern invention. It is found in the *Anguttara Nikāya*, and is therefore as ancient as that collection. It also occurs in the Abidharma. Its appearance, therefore, in this Northern copy of the Vinaya may not be used as an argument to prove the late redaction of the Dharmagupta Scriptures; on the contrary, it confirms the opinion expressed by Mr. Morris that the division referred to is more ancient than is generally supposed.

We conclude by reminding our readers that the first Buddhist council is now believed to be fabulous. Dr. Oldenberg in his preface to his edition of the Vinaya Piṭaka, has pretty well established this, but, at the same time, he shows that the account cannot be dated much later than 400 B.C. This date is

---

1 Idam pi te âvuso Ânanda dukkaṭaṃ yaṃ tvaṃ matugâmehi bhagavato sarîram paṭhamam vandâpesi, tâsaṃ rodantinaṃ bhagavato sarîraṃ assukena makkhitaṃ (Oldenberg, p. 289).

2 In the Sarvastavadin version, instead of Lo-pi'en (*Rabbin*), we find "Sse" = *Master*.

3 The Angel Messias, by E. de Bunsen, p. 87.

4 *Academy*, August 21, 1880, p. 136.

sufficiently remote to make the record interesting to all those who wish to search out the origin of Buddhist doctrine and ritual.

I now proceed to give an account of the second Council, which is without doubt historical; the study will be thus more complete, and the comparison between the documents in the North and South more exact.

The Council of the Seven Hundred.

[School of the Dharmaguptas.]

At this time, the world-honoured one having attained Nirvāna a hundred years, the Vajjiputra Bhikshus of Vesāli practised ten indulgences, saying they were in agreement with the pure laws of Buddha, to wit, two fingers measuring food; between villages; within the Temple; to make after-binding-laws; to use agreeable (mixtures with food); to use salt during a night's rest; to drink jalogi (che-lau-lo wine); of seats without fringes; of receiving gold and silver on the Uposatha days from patrons and afterwards dividing the proceeds.

At this time there was (a disciple) called Yasa the son of Kana, who heard that the Vesāli Bhikshus were acting in this way. On this he forthwith went to the place where dwelt the Vajjiputra Bhikshus, and witnessed their proceedings, to wit, the way in which they exhorted their patrons on Uposatha days to give to the Sañgha silver and gold, and then the way in which they divided the contributions, and exclaimed "that a fair proportion should be given to Yasa the son of Kana." On this he cried out, "I will receive nothing of these contributions. For why? No Shaman who is a Śākyaputra should ever accept either gold or silver. No Śākyaputra should ever adorn himself with pearl or precious stone."

And then, on another day, when they again offered him his proportion of the gifts, he said, "I formerly declared that no Shaman who was a Śākyaputra was allowed to accept any precious thing for personal adornment." On this they replied, "The Upasaka disciples of Vesāli are much annoyed with you; you ought to go and instruct them and cause them joy." And further, they sent to him certain disciples who should accompany him to the place where the Upasakas dwelt. Arriving there, he addressed them as follows: "Are you really vexed with me because I said that no Shaman who was a Śākyaputra ought to accept gold or silver as a gift, or any precious thing for personal adornment?" And then he spake further on this wise, and said, "When the world-honoured was residing at Rājagriha, there were assembled in the king's palace all the great ministers, who spake thus and said, 'Is it lawful for the Shamans, disciples of Śākya (Śākyaputras), to accept gold and silver, and ought they to reject pearls and precious stones intended for personal adornment?'

"And then in the midst of the assembly there was a certain noble called Maṇisûlako, who addressed the assembled ministers as follows: 'Pray say not that the Shamans Śākyaputras may accept gold and silver, and also pearls and precious stones for personal adornment. For why? They ought not indeed to accept these things.'

"And then Maṇisûlako continued his address on account of the assembled ministers and said (as before), causing them to accept with joy and gladness his declaration.

"After this Maṇisûlako, the nobleman, went to the place where the world-honoured one was residing, and having saluted him (embraced his foot), took a seat on one side, and spoke thus according to the previous circumstances: 'I declared so and so to be in agreement with the sacred will of the honoured of the world.'

"Buddha replied, 'Noble sir! it is as you say; this is the will and commandment of the Holy One, to wit, that no disciple of mine should ever accept gold or silver or precious things for personal adornment; they who receive these things do indeed also accept (the permission to enjoy) the five (sensual) pleasures, and they can in no sense be my disciples. My only permission is, that they may procure bamboo shoots and wood by means of money, but not in any case by them to be received.' Therefore, O Litchavis! according to this sentence the Shamans who are disciples ought not to accept gold or silver, &c.

"And again at another time, when the world-honoured was residing in the Jetavana, he addressed his followers in this way:

'There are four reasons, O Bhikshus! why the sun and the moon do not emit their splendour, and what are the four? First, (the giant) Rahu, then the clouds, and then the mists, and afterwards the dust which arises from the earth. These are the four things which obscure the brightness of the sun and the moon; and so there are four things which obscure the life of Shaman and Brahman and defile it, viz., drinking wine, and a habit of it; lust, and a habit of it; love of pelf, and a habit of it; fondness of strange doctrine, and a habit of it. These four things obscure the life and hide the lustre of the Brahman and Shaman.' And then the world-honoured one added these verses and said—

"'The pollution of lust (covetousness and lust)
Affecting the Shaman or Brahman,
The clouds of ignorance which cover him,
Love of external emblems of beauty,
Fondness for wine, leading to confusion of mind—
These are the incitements to evil desire.
Accepting gold and silver and precious stones,
This is the mark of an ignorant man—
(Mark) of the Shaman or Brahman
Who has joined himself to a system of false doctrine.
Buddha says that these things
Are as the clouds that obscure the sun's light,
Which envelop it with darkness
And hide its native purity;
These are the bonds of ignorance and blindness,
This power of lust and desire,
Constraining to evil ways and not to good,
This delusion of sense which leads the steps
Onward through the tangled way of sin,
And causes the repetition of endless births.

"'By this, then, O Litchavis! and from this argument, you ought to know that no Shaman who is a Śākyaputra may accept either gold or silver, or anything calculated for personal adornment. Are you convinced by what I say that I am right or not?'

"Then the Litchavis replied, 'Far be it from us to disbelieve what you say; on the contrary, we rejoice to place reliance in your teaching, and we pray you to remain in this (town of) Vesāli, and we will provide you with food and drink, clothes and medicaments, and whatever other things you need.'"

Then Kanaputra the Bhikshu having by his explanation of duty caused the Litchavis to rejoice, returned in company with the Bhikshu messengers to the Vajjiputra Bhikshus; these, perceiving the approach of Kanaputra Bhikshu, immediately addressed the messenger priests and said, "Have the Litchavi princes accepted the teaching of Kanaputra and put faith in it?" Replying, they said, "Yea, they have believed, and Kanaputra has declared that we are no Shamans, sons of Śākya." "And in what way has he proved this?" they inquired; and then the messengers related the previous portion of the narrative. On this those Vesā hikshus addressed Kanaputra Bhikshu and said, "You have committed an offence by your previous slander of the Sañgha." To this he replied, "I have not slandered the assembly." They then having agreed to join together for the purpose of discussing the question and passing sentence against Kanaputra, he reflected, "This is a troublesome quarrel. I must secure the venerable Revata to hold with me, that we may be able to suppress this schism." He asked, therefore, of some indifferent person, "Where is Revata now living?" Who replied, "I hear he is living at *P'o-ho-ho-pien*."[1] Going there, Revata was not in that place. Again he inquired, "Where does Revata now dwell?" Whereupon one answered, "He is dwelling in the Ki'a-na-wei-ché (Kannakujja?) country." Having gone there, he found Revata had taken his departure. He inquired once more, "Where does Revata now dwell?" To whom one replied, "He is now living in the country called Ho-ki'a-lau-to (Aggalapura). Going there, he again found Revata had departed, on which he once more inquired, "Where dwells Revata at present?" To which one answered, "He is in the Sang-ki'a-she (Saṃkassa) country." Going there, finding the followers of Revata assembled together, on which he inquired of one of them, "Does your venerable master, Revata, dwell with you or not?" To whom he replied, "He has just gone." Now Revata had gone that night to recite

[1] Is this Ahogañga, or is it *Pupphapura*?—*Vide* Mahawanso, p. 17.

the law (preach) in the midst of his followers, and having done so, just after midnight he had gathered up his sitting-mat and returned home. On this, Yasa, having also gone to the assembly and heard the law preached, also gathered up his sitting-mat and went to the place where Revata dwelt. Then Yasa reflected, "This is a good occasion for detailing the circumstances before related," and so he addressed Revata as follows:—

"Reverend sir (Mahâbhadanta) Sthavira! is it permitted or not with two fingers to take food?" He answered in reply and said, "What is this taking food with two fingers?" In answer he said, "Having had sufficient food (if a priest), neglecting the rules relating to decorous conduct which forbid him to take other (remnants) food, with two fingers take fragments of food to eat (this is the case alluded to)."[1] Revata replied, "It is unlawful." Yasa inquired, "In what place was the law made binding?" He answered, "At Srâvasti, when the rules respecting further (or remaining) food were enacted, this also was forbidden."

Again he asked, "Most reverend and venerable sir! is between villages' lawful?" He answered in reply, "What is this 'between villages'?" He answered, "Most reverend and venerable sir! having obtained sufficient food (if a priest), neglecting the decorous rules which relate to not receiving other food, when between two villages take other food and eat it (this is the case alluded to)." Revata replied, "It is not lawful." He then asked where the rule was enacted. Revata replied, "At Srâvasti, when the laws were framed which relate to receiving 'other food,' this was also made binding."

Again he inquired, "Most reverend and venerable sir! is 'within the temple' allowable?" He answered and said, "What is this 'within the Temple' permission?" He answered, "Most reverend and venerable sir! this refers to the practice of convening within the Temple other Sañghakammas (than the regular ones)." Revata replied, "It is not lawful . . . and the law was passed at Rajâgriha among the Upasotha khandhakas."[2]

---

[1] In the Sarvastavadina Vinaya it is said, "If a priest, rising from his seat, after having taken sufficient food, pick up with two fingers the fragments lying about," &c.

[2] For Khandhaka *vide* Childers' Dict., sub. voc. *Vinayo.*

Again he asked, "Most reverend and venerable sir! is 'after permission' allowable or not?"[1] He replied, "What is this 'after permission'?" He said, "Most reverend and venerable sir! whilst dwelling within the 'sacred precinct,' having assembled an irregular Sañghakamma, is it permissible to act on their decision?" Revata answered, "It is not permissible, as was enacted (as before)."

Again he asked, "Is it right to have 'ever-during laws'?" In reply Revata inquired, "What is the meaning of 'ever-during laws'?" He answered, "Most reverend and venerable sir! this refers to the case of those who, having done a thing, sanction their conduct by saying, 'So it was from the beginning.'" He replied, "Whatever is not found in the Sûtras, the Vinaya, or the Rules of Prohibition (*kin kiau fă liu*), ought not to be done."[2]

Again he asked, "Most reverend and venerable sir! is 'sweet (mixture)' right?" He replied, "What is sweet (mixture)?" He said, "Most reverend and venerable sir! the priests having partaken of sufficient food, in contradiction to the rules respecting additional food, taking a mixture of butter and honey, or that which is produced from butter,[3] or a mixture of candied honey (sugar-candy?) and milk, and so making an agreeable compound, drink it. This is the case alluded to." Revata replied, "It is not allowable, as was determined at Srâvasti among the rules relating to superfluous food."

Again he asked, "Most reverend and venerable sir! is salt-mixing for one night lawful?" He replied, "What is salt-mixing for one night?" He answered, "Most reverend and venerable sir! the use of salt for preserving food during a night, and afterwards eating it—this is the case alluded to." Revata said, "It is not lawful, as was determined at Srâvasti among the Khandhaka rules relating to medicine."

Again he asked, "Most reverend and venerable sir! is it lawful to drink *che-lau-lo* (jalogi) wine?" Revata answered, "It is not lawful, as was determined at Kausambi in the case of the venerable Bhikshu *Sha-kĭa-to* (Sakata?)"

[1] Does this correspond with "samāna-sīmā" of the Pāli?

[2] This is a mere explanation of the original, which is obscure.

[3] I suppose, corresponds with the Pali "khirabhavam."

He inquired again, "Most reverend and venerable sir! is it allowable to obtain and keep untrimmed sitting cushions?" He answered, "It is not lawful, as was determined at Srâvasti in the case of the six bodies of Bhikshus (or the body of Bhikshus six in number, *sambahulá bhikkhú*)."

Again he asked, "Most reverend and venerable sir! is it lawful to receive gold and silver or not?" He replied, "It is not lawful, as was determined at Râjagriha, on account of *Balandá*[1] Śākyaputra."

He then said, "Most reverend and venerable sir! the Vajjiputra Bhikshus of Vesāli practise these ten indulgences, and say that they are admissible according to the law of Buddha. They moreover exhort their patrons (dánapatis) on Uposatha days to bestow upon the Sañgha gold and silver, and cause them to divide among them goods of different kinds (or 'that they may be able to divide,' *i.e.*, that the money may purchase goods). After division they say, 'Tell no one what has been done, lest the Bhikshus who agree not with us cause discord.'"

(Revata said),[2] "Go thou to Mount Ahóganga, and there you will find the Bhikshu Sambuto, who is my fellow-disciple, of the same spiritual-teacher[3] (Upádhyáya), with sixty Bhikshus, sons of P'o-lo-li (Patheyá?);[4] all these are eminent for their advance in the Paramita of perseverance (virya), delivered from fear; for this reason, when you have addressed them, let them all assemble by the side of this river Po-ho, where I also will go."

At which time, Yasa the son of Kana, the Bhikshu, proceeded forthwith to that mount, to the place where Sambuto was, and having spoken to him according to the above tenor, invited him to proceed to the banks of the river Po-ho to meet Revata there.

At this time the Vajjiputta Bhikshus of Vesāli hearing that Yasa Bhikshu, the son of Kana, had gone out among men to look for associates (to co-operate with him), forthwith proceeded to the place where the disciple of Revata dwelt, taking with them costly garments (made at) Vesāli. Arriving there, they

---

[1] *Po-man-to;* it may be *Upananda.*

[2] I supply this as it seems to be necessary.

[3] *I.e.*, of Ananda.

[4] Vide, *Mahawanso*, p. 16.

said, "We have brought these goodly clothes for the very reverend Revata for his acceptance; pray receive them as we respectfully present them." He replied, "Stop! stop! I cannot receive them." But on their beseeching and urging him, he was induced to accept them.

Having accepted them, they further addressed him as follows: "Reverend sir! the Bhikshus of the two countries of Po-i-na and Po-li (Pâcînakâ va bbhikkû Pâṭheyyakâ vâ 'ti) are contending together; now the world-honoured Buddha whilst alive dwelt (for some time) in the Po-i-na country. Well, reverend sir, we desire you to acquaint the venerable Sthavira (Revata) of these things [repeating them], so that he may succour the Bhikshus of the Po-i-na country."

The other immediately replied, saying, "The venerable and reverend Revata forbids his disciples giving any opinion on doubtful matters."

They pressed the question still, but without gaining their end, on which they went to the place where Revata was and addressed him thus: "Reverend sir! the Bhikshus of the Po-i-na country are at difference with those of the Po-li country. Now the world-honoured Buddha belonged to the Po-i-na country; we pray you, therefore, reverend sir, to give your aid to the Bhikshus of that country."

Revata immediately answered, saying, "You are ignorant men to think that I would hold with anything of an impure (erroneous) character in any school of teaching (or with any erroneous school). You may go! I have no further need of you."

Having thus received their dismissal, they went back to Vesāli, to the place where dwelt the Vajjiputra Bhikshus, and one of them spoke thus to them: "Reverend sirs! I said beforehand to you that the venerable (*ta tih*) Revata was very difficult to deal with, and we were unable to speak boldly before him. Now we greatly fear there is mischief in store for us."

On this those Bhikshus replied, "Why do you think so?" They said, "Because he sent us away so abruptly."

They again said, "How many years have you been in the fraternity?" [1] He said, "Twelve years."

[1] *La* for *varsha*.

They answered, "And was it not a disgrace that you should thus be dismissed (or were you not ashamed to be so sent away) after being twelve years ordained?"

He answered, "But he would not receive our religious offerings; how then could we help feeling afraid?"

And now Revata and the Bhikshus who were with him spake thus together, "We ought now to go to the place where this contention has arisen." Embarking, therefore, in a boat on the Ganges, they set forth. At this time during the very great heat they drew the boat up near the shore and halted awhile in the shade.

At this time there was a venerable person named Vâsabhagâmika[1] going on the road, and as he went reflecting thus: "Now then, with respect to this contention about matters, I will just look at the Sûtras and Vinaya to see who is right and who is wrong." Accordingly he looked into the Sûtras and the Vinaya and the Prohibitory Rules, and then he saw that the Bhikshus of the Po-li country were right, and the Bhikshus of the Po-i-na country were wrong. At this time a Deva, whose form was invisible, uttered these laudatory stanzas, and said, "Well done, illustrious youth! it is as you apprehend; the Po-li Bhikshus are right, the Po-i-na Bhikshus are wrong."

And now all the venerable ones proceeded onwards to Vesāli. At this time there was at Vesāli an eminent (chang-lau) disciple whose name was *Yih-tsai-hu* (Sabbakâmî); he was the principal Sthavira in all Jambudwipa. On this Sambuto thus addressed Revata, saying, "Let us now go to the abode of the Sthavira Sabbakâmî and lodge for the night, that we may talk over these things together." On this the two went to the abode of Sâbbakâmî. On arriving there, they found him absorbed in night-contemplation. And now the night was passing by, when Revata thought thus with himself, "This Sthavira, although old, and the power of his vital spirits (*hi*) waning, is able to sit for so long as this in contemplation. How much more ought I to do so, according to his example." Then Revata forthwith sat himself down and occupied himself in severe reflection.

[1] Ch. *Po-san-tsim.*

And so the night wore on, when Sabbakâmî thought thus, "This stranger priest has come from far, and although worn and weary, still persists in ecstatic contemplation; how much more ought I to persevere in mine?" and so the venerable sage still sat on, engaged in deep thought.

And now the night was passed, and they engaged in conversation. Addressing Revata, Sabbakâmî said, "Venerable sir! what system of religion (fă) has engaged your mind during your contemplation to-night?"

Answering, he replied, "Formerly when I was a white-clothed (Upâsaka, a layman), I constantly cultivated a 'loving heart;' this night, during my moments of deep thought, I entered the Samâdhi called *love* (*tsz*)." On this Sabbakâmî answered, "You have occupied yourself in a minor sort of Samâdhi (*siu teng*) to-night, for such is this Samâdhi of love."

And now Revata inquired, "And in what have you been engaged during your contemplation?"

He answered, "When I was formerly a white-clothed disciple, I engaged myself in investigating the 'Law of Emptiness,' and to-night I have been absorbed in the 'Samâdhi of Emptiness.'"

The other said, "You have been engaged in a Samâdhi appropriate to a great man."

And then he thought, this is now a good opportunity for entering on the questions under consideration. He therefore addressed Sabbakâmî and said, "Most reverend and venerable sir! is it lawful to take two fingers or not?" [Questions and answers just as before.]

Sabbakâmî was now the first Sthavira in the world, Sambuno (Sambuto?) the second, Revata the third, and Vasabhagamika the fourth. All these were related alike to Ananda as their Upâdhyâya.[1]

Forthwith the venerable Sabbakâmî addressed (the assembled Sañgha and) said, "Venerable priests, listen! If the priests will now hear me, let them patiently attend! The Sañgha is now about to go over the Dhammavinaya and give its assent;" (say, "So it is.")

On this the *Po-i-na* Bhikshus addressed the *Po-li* Bhikshus

[1] Teacher or preceptor.

and said, "You ought to select a certain (equal) number of men (to represent you)." Forthwith they named the Sthavira Sabbakâmî, Revata, Yasa, and Sumana. The Po-li Bhikshus then addressed the Po-i-na Bhikshus in the same way, on which they selected the venerable Sambuto, Vâsabhâgâmika, the venerable Salha, and Pacchesuma (Khujjasobhita?).

Now, amongst the number of assembled persons there was a certain Bhikshu called Ajita,[1] who earnestly addressed the other Bhikshus in these words: "Keep these Bhikshus in our midst, my friends, for their business concerns us; we ought therefore to be in one place together, and therefore I exhort you to do so."

Then those Sthaviras reflected thus: "If we remain in the assembly, various questions will be asked and further strife stirred up;" and therefore they thought, "To what spot shall we adjourn to settle these matters?" and finally they moved that they should go to the Po-li grove (Vâlikârâmo).

Then the venerable Sabbakâmî spoke as follows: "Venerable sirs! listen; with reference to this matter, if it is convenient to the Sañgha, let them patiently attend. We purpose to go over the Dhammavinaya in the Vâlikârâmo grove, and in the absence of the rest to assent to what is recited (or the contrary), and having done so, then by the selection of the congregation, two or three of the Sañgha may join themselves with us in the Vâlikârâmo grove (as a deputation?) to join in the after consultation." Thus it was Sabbakâmî addressed the assembled Bhikshus.

Then the Sthaviras afore named adjourned to the Vâlikârâmo grove, and Sabbakâmî addressed them as follows: "Reverend priests! listen; if it is now convenient, let the priests patiently attend. We will now go over the Dhammavinaya whilst the priests give their assent."

Then Revata spoke thus: "Reverend brethren! listen; if the time is a suitable one, let the priests patiently attend, and whilst I ask Sabbakâmî respecting the Dhammavinaya, let the priests give their assent." Then Sabbakâmî again spoke, "Reverend sirs! let the priests listen, &c.; let Revata

[1] O-i-tau.

question me whilst I answer whether the Dhammavinaya is so or not."

Then Revata addressed Sabbakâmî saying, "Most reverend Sthavira! is it lawful to take 'two fingers' or not?" He answered, "Explain the meaning of 'two fingers,'" [and so on as before]. (In reply to all which Sabbakâmî replies that it is not lawful, nor according to the Dhammavinaya.)

The Sthaviras having all agreed to the determination of Sabbakâmî, they again adjourn to Vesāli, and there, in the presence of the whole congregation, recite the law respecting the ten transgressions [as before], and according to the provisions of the Dhammavinaya each fault is exposed, and the contrary made binding on the community.

(The Assembly of the Seven Hundred at Vesāli, to determine the provisions of the Dhammavinaya in relation to certain indulgences.)

LECTURE III.

ASVAGHOSHA.

AMONG the distinguished Buddhists who lived about the time of Kanishka (the Indo-Skythian conqueror of North India), the twelfth Buddhist patriarch, Asvaghosha, was not the least so. It is now tolerably certain[1] that Kanishka's reign began about 78 A.D. It is not strange, then, if we find in Asvaghosha's writings many allusions and illustrations derived apparently from foreign, and perhaps Christian, sources. To me, indeed, it appears, if the date above named be the true one, that much in the Buddhist development coming under the name of the Greater Vehicle may be explained on this ground.

With respect to Asvaghosha, we find from a notice in a biographical work (the *Lai-tai-san-paou-ki*, vol. i. p. 13), that he was a native of Eastern India and of the Brahman caste, and having been converted to Buddhism, he did his best to overthrow the system of the Brahmans. There is a brief memoir of him also in a Chinese work written by Kumârajiva. According to this author, he was a disciple of Parsva. The latter (who was president of the Council held under Kanishka), having gone from North India to Central India, found that the Buddhist clergy were afraid to sound the gong, that is, were unable to challenge their opponents to discuss questions of difference. The cause of this humiliation was Asvaghosha, who belonged to the best instructed of the heretics (Tirtikas), and had by his superior skill silenced the Buddhists. Parsva ordered it to be sounded, and entered into dispute with Asvaghosha. In consequence the latter became a disciple of Parsva, who advised him to study Buddhism, and

[1] Compare Fergusson's *Saka, Samvat, and Gupta Eras*, with Dr. Oldenberg in the *Zeitschrift für Numismatik*, vol. viii.

afterwards returned to his own country. Asvaghosha remained in Mid-India and rendered himself conspicuous for his superior talents. The king of the Little Yue-chi (*i.e.*, Kanishka) having invaded Magadha, demanded from the people the cups (begging-dishes) of Buddha and Asvaghosha; the inhabitants murmured, thinking that the king valued the latter at too high a price. But the king, to show his right estimation of Asvaghosha's merit, selected seven horses, and after keeping them without food for six days, he took them to the place where Asvaghosha was preaching, and ordered forage to be given them; but the horses, instead of eating, shed tears on hearing the words of the preacher and refused the food. Asvaghosha therefore became celebrated because the horses understood his voice, and hence he was called "The voice of the horse"—Asvaghosha.

This is the account of Kumârajiva, translated probably from an original Life of the patriarchs *Nagarjuna*, *Aryadeva*, and *Asvaghosha*. We may remark, however, that the Mahâyanists make Asvaghosha a disciple of *Aryadeva* and not of Parsva, the former being a convert of Nagârjuna and a native of Ceylon. But in any case, the date of Asvaghosha will not be affected much by this explanation, as Nagârjuna, if any reliable date can be given to him, lived not far from the time of Kanishka. We have some small additional information respecting Asvaghosha in a communication made by the late Archimandrite Paladii; it is found in the second vol. (pp. 156 ff.) of the Memoranda of the Russian Mission at Pekin (quoted[1] by Weber). From this we find that Asvaghosha was an historical person who lived in the time of Kanishka; he was, with Nagarjuna, the founder of the Mahâyana system of Buddhism, and afterwards, in conjunction with Bodhisatwa, *i.e.*, Aryadeva, opened the way to the spread of the Yogâchârya school. He flourished at Benares. He was renowned for his acquaintance with the Vedas and the six Shasters, which were used in the six schools of the Brahmans, and also with the Vyâkaranas, or the treatises on the meaning of words. He was a renowned dialectician, so that no one could stand before him in argument. He was a Pantheist—that is, he maintained

[1] Die Vajrasûçî des Açvaghosha, p. 259.

that a common principle of life was found in man, the inferior world of animals, and even in herbs and grass. He defeated the Buddhists in all disputations, and finally silenced them. He was finally converted by Parsva.

We are told by the same writer that Asvaghosha was a poet and musician, and that he travelled about with a troup of music-men and women, and was successful by these means in bringing about the conversion of a Rajâputra and others. He finally took up his abode in Kashmir. His principal work was a Life of Buddha in verse, the Buddhacharita, which is still known to us through a Chinese version.

The only other notice of Asvaghosha alluded to by Weber is a short extract from the Tandjur of Thibet, in which a mere list of his works is given. I need not name these; they are eight in number. I will, however, briefly refer to one of them. This is the *Life of Buddha*, written in verse, called in Hodgson's list the "*Buddhacharita*," and also the Mahâkâvya or Great Poem. According to Burnouf, p. 556 (*Int. B.*), it is composed in verse, the metre being Anushtub and Indravajra, that is, verses of eight syllables and eleven syllables respectively. The style, Burnouf adds, if not very poetic, is at least correct and perfectly intelligible. It is a substantive abridgment of the Lalita Vistara; and this circumstance deserves more notice, as there are not observable in the work of Asvaghosha any peculiarities derived from Pāli or the Prakrits. Hence, he says, we are sure that the *Buddhacharita* is a work posterior to the Lalita Vistara, as it is written in a language more grammatically correct. He adds that there is no authority for supposing the author of this work to be the celebrated patriarch of the same name, and he conjectures that it may have been written by the author of the *Vajrasuchî*.

But we have evidence (contrary to Burnouf's opinion) in the Chinese copy of this work that the patriarch Asvaghosha was the compiler of it, for it is expressly referred to him by the translator, Dharmâkshaya, who was a native of Mid-India, and flourished in China about the beginning of the fifth century of our era. The title of the book as so translated is this — "*Fo-sho-hing-tsan*," *i.e.*, laudatory verses embracing the life (conduct) of Buddha, compiled by the

Bodhisatwa Maming, i.e., Asvaghosha, and translated by *Tan-mo-tsich* of the North Liang dynasty, an Indian, and a master of the three Piṭakas. In passing I may notice there is another Life of Buddha extant in China, which is also composed in stanzas. It is commonly called the *Fo-pen-hing-king,* and also known as the *Fo-pen-hing-tsan-king.* From internal evidence this work appears to be another version of Asvaghosha's *Buddha-charita,* although in some material points it differs from it; as, *e.g.,* in the number and heading of the chapters. But, on the other hand, it is composed in verses of varying length, some of four, others of five, and some of seven syllables (symbols) to a line. This agrees with Burnouf's description of the Sanscrit copy of Asvaghosha's composition, and so far tends to show that the Chinese possess two versions of the work—the first (named before) translated by Dharmâkshaya in the early part of the fifth century, the second translated by Ratnamegha [1] of the Sung dynasty.

I shall now proceed to give a list of the chapters of the *Buddhacharita,* translated by Dharmâkshaya, with a view to a comparison with any Sanscrit copy that may be available in India or Europe.

THE FO-SHO-HING-TSAN-KING IN FIVE KIOUEN.

KIOUEN I.

	Pages
§ 1. Origin of race, ...	1–9
§ 2. Occupies the palace, ...	9–13
§ 3. Filled with sorrow (on account of sufferings he witnessed), ...	13–18
§ 4. Gives up a life of pleasure, ...	18–22
§ 5. Leaves the city, ...	22–29

KIOUEN II.

§ 6. Return of Tchandaka, ...	1–6
§ 7. Enters the forest of suffering (Uravilva), . . .	6–11
§ 8. The grief when he (Tchandaka) enters the palace on his return, ...	11–17
§ 9. Mission dispatched to search for the royal prince, .	17–25

[1] Ratnamegha (Gem-cloud) was a companion of Fa-hien in his travels, and a native of China.

Kiouen III.

Kiouen IV.

Kiouen V.

By way of comparison I will also give the headings of the chapters of the *Fo-pen-hing-king*, which, as I have before stated, is written in verse of varied measures, but is not attributed to Asvaghosha. It was translated into Chinese, as I have just said, by Ratnamegha, who flourished shortly before the time of Dharmâkshaya, *i.e.*, the end of the fourth century A.D.

THE FO-PEN-HING-KING IN SEVEN KIOUEN.

KIOUEN I.

KIOUEN II.

KIOUEN III.

KIOUEN IV.

KIOUEN V.

Kiouen VI.

Kiouen VII.

Let me now allude to another work, which I have already named, written by Asvaghosha, viz., the *Mahâlamkâra Sûtra Shastra.* This book was translated into Chinese by Kumārajiva about A.D. 410. Originally (as the Encyclopædia *Lai-tai-san-paou-ki* states) it was in ten kiouen, but the work before me is in thirteen kiouen. From the eleventh to the thirteenth kiouen appear to have been added at a later date.

This work consists of a series of sermons or narratives sixty-six in number, of an instructive character. It is evidently the work of a partisan, opposed to Brahmanism, yet intimately acquainted with its literature; and such a writer, according all accounts, was Asvaghosha.

The following is a list of these sermons :—

LIST OF TEXTS

In illustration of which stories or traditional records are related, found in the thirteen Kiouen of the Ta-chwang-yan-king-lun.

1. The three gems.
2. Right distinction of religious teaching.
3. In affairs of religion no differences of persons or ages to be considered.
4. The advantage of hearing the law explained is so great that the most sinful may be converted.
5. The non-covetous are those who, although they possess great possessions, do not set their heart and affections on them.

6. The disobedient are those who pretend to keep the law, but act from interested motives.
7. In following erroneous doctrine there is much affliction, but in obeying the truth much gain.
8. True independence results not from mere words or bodily discipline, but from right government of the thoughts.
9. The truly wise man covets not wealth.
10. The contented man, although poor, is counted rich. The discontented man, though rich, is counted poor.
11. All men honour the professor of religion who scrupulously observes the rules of religious conduct.
12. The man inwardly pure has great peace; all wise persons therefore cultivate inward purity.
13. Escape from the sorrows of birth and death does not result from much hearing, but from an inward perception of the truth (traces of religion).
14. On the inconstancy of all earthly possessions and dignities.
15. It is impossible to carry our wealth into the next world; it is only by using our possessions in charity that poverty in the next world can be provided against.
16. Our present condition as men is uncertain and changeable, the wise man, therefore, regards with reverence all persons who deserve reverence, without distinction of person.
17. Fault is not to be found unnecessarily.
18. Against carelessness.
19. Those who are without faults of their own may reprove others, but if a man guilty of the same crime reproves another for it, he only provokes laughter against himself.
20. If a man, without any selfish love, is able to give away all he has in charity, then his name becomes great indeed.
21. If a person in his charitable offerings acts from a supreme principle of faith, then two mites thus offered secures an incalculable reward.
22. If a man living among his friends has one who is able to govern his heart and regulate his conduct aright, this is a true friend indeed.
23. If a man, in consequence of his evil deeds, is ready to perish (fall into hell), if he has a friend who can correct the evil, he may, by his means, obtain birth in heaven.
24. He who gives his possessions away in charity avoids the danger of the eight calamities (fire, disease, &c.); but he who heaps

up his wealth is in constant danger of these. The wise man gives away in charity, and this is his stronghold.

25. He who hears the truth declared, is able to escape the fetters (of error).

26. When a person is sick, his words have but little force and are not attended to.

27. A wise man never resents with passion the abuse of the foolish.

28. The concerns of the body are like the illusive movements of an apparitional body.

29. By discoursing on the duty of charity, the germ of virtue is quickened, and then the deeper matters of religion may be considered.

30. Reverence may be paid to that which deserves reverence, but it is the destruction of that which has no such claim.

31. A man who has once made religious inquiries, though he fall away, may yet be recovered by the recollection of what he has heard.

32. He who would lay up a virtuous reward for the future must now diligently practise virtue.

33. All men seek their own profit; some find what they seek, others not; but the man whose purpose is a true one and not a selfish one obtains true profit.

34. Evil desires (bonds) must be entirely eradicated, or else they will, when occasion offers, assert their power, even as ice will, when violently struck, emit fire.

35. Charity must be practised not for reward, but for the purpose of final release.

36. It is difficult to remove all the obstacles which prevent our possessing a human form; but even when born as a man, every effort ought to be used to remove all obstacles.

37. It is difficult to learn to part with the least of one's wealth; the wise man despises not even the least exercise of a charitable disposition.

38. A man considering his actions in a right spirit, although he finds faults in his conduct (or suffers loss), yet afterwards reaps profit.

39. Selfish charity (done for personal profit) is destructive of all religious progress (?).

40. Shortcomings may be prevented by a mode of teaching intelligible to the person concerned.

41. The root of violence, though sometimes deadened, will revive again through the mercy of Tathâgata.
42. A disciple should persevere in his religious duties, though he fail at first to see the truth.
43. The words of Buddha are alone sufficient to heal diseases of mind and body; we ought, therefore, to persevere in listening to the law.
44. It is better to sacrifice life than transgress our convictions of duty.
45. A proud heart leads to a vicious life.
46. He who has once seen the truth cannot be induced to speak against it by all the temptations of Mâra or the arguments of heretics.
47. Unless the mind has acquired settled faith, there can be no composure at the end of life.
48. Charity is always due to the true disciple. The wise man regards the obedient as a true disciple (whatever his caste).
49. The instruction of Buddha is useless in the case of those whose minds are filled with angry passions. The wise man, therefore, avoids anger.
50. Right examination of food is necessary, and therefore Buddha enacted rules respecting food.
51. Lustful desire is an ungovernable madness.
52. Buddha perceiving that, after a time, a believing heart may be formed, therefore did nothing quickly.
53. The advantage of reciting the praises of Buddha securing the reverence of men.
54. The great advantage of charity on the part of those who have no pre-eminent position.
55. The most unworthy who seeks for salvation is not to be forbidden.
56. When the root of virtue is properly matured, then salvation is at hand. We ought, therefore, to cultivate the root of virtue.
57. As men sow they shall reap.
58. If a seed produces fruit, it is not attributable to good luck; how much less then is there any sound reason in taking lucky signs?
59. If a man of small wisdom is moved by the outward signs of Buddha's person to a religious life, how much more should the eminently wise be so moved by considering the same?

60. A great man seeks not the charity of the indifferent, but the reverence of those who offer charity.
61. Better lay down one's life than break a commandment.
62. The law of Buddha is difficult to hear. In old time Bodhisatwa did not grudge his life in trying to fulfil the law; we ought then diligently to listen to that law.
63. A true friend is one who can deliver a man from (moral) servitude.
64. The great profit of rendering worship to a Stûpa.
65. Though a man has had a good foundation of religion laid, yet he may fall into hell by neglecting to hear the law.

As a specimen of Asvaghosha's teaching, I will here produce a translation of the introductory sermons of this series.

THE TA-CHWANG-YĂN-KING-LUN.

KIOUEN I.

Written by Asvaghosha Bodhisatwa (circ. 70 A.D.), and translated by Kumārajiva (circ. 400 A.D.), a Doctor of the three Pitakas.

PREFATORY STANZAS.

First I adore the supremely excellent Lord,
Who has freed himself from lust and mounted above the three worlds.
I also reverence the all-wise,
Eternal, superlative Law,
And with these the eightfold assembly,
The spotless, incontaminate Church.
The mendicants Puṇyayasas and Parsvika,[1]
All the doctors of the Mahisasakas,[2]
The assembly of the Sarvastavadins,[3]

---

[1] The original has simply "Punna and Hie, Bhikshus." I restore *Punna* to Puṇyayasas, and *Hie* to Parsvika. These two were the tenth and eleventh patriarchs of the Buddhist Church, Asvaghosha being the twelfth. Eitel, in his *Handbook* (p. 98, c. 2), states that Puṇyayasas laboured in Benares and converted Asvaghosha.

[2] *Chinese*, Mi-chi.

[3] *Chinese*, Sa-po-shih-po.

True disciples of the King of Oxen,[1]
All these true learned masters,[2]
I reverence and follow equally.
Now I am going to declare in order
The *Hien-tsung-chwang-yăn* Shastra,[3]
That those hearing it may obtain in their fulness
The good things resulting herefrom.
Let all, whether professors of faith or not,
Whether members of the congregation or not,[4]
Whethér excellent (good) or evil,[5]
Let them all distinguish what is said.

It was reported long ago that some merchantmen of the country of Kien-to-lo (Gândhâra) in their journeyings arrived at the country of Ma-tu (Mathura). Now there was in that country a Stûpa of Buddha. Among the merchants was one, a Upâsaka, who one day went to that sacred building to worship and adore. Now as he thus worshipped there passed along the road certain Brahmans, who, seeing the Upâsaka worshipping the tower of Buddha, all of them began to jeer and laugh at him. Again, on another day, when the weather was very hot, these Brahmans, after their daily meal, went forth to stroll, and were scattered here and there. Some loitered along the road, others sat beside the different gates, some were bathing, others anointing themselves, some walking, others sitting. Now at this time the Upâsaka happened to be returning after worshipping at the Pagoda. Then the Brahmans seeing him cried out and said, "Come here, Upâsaka! come here and sit down." Having taken a seat, they spoke to him in these words: "How is it you know not of our Maheśvara and Vishnu and our other gods, whom you ought to worship, and not trouble yourself about honouring this Tower of Buddha?"

[1] *Nieou-wang-ching-tao-ché;* the translation is difficult. I assume that the "King of the Oxen" is *Gotama.* It may, however, be simply rendered "leader" or "chief" (*Gopati*).

[2] Masters of Treatises (*lun*).

[3] If restored, these characters would stand for *Prakaraṇa śâsana alamkâra shastra.*

[4] This and the preceding line may mean "whether cleric or laymen."

[5] Or, "whether high or low."

Then the Upâsaka answered at once and said, "I know some small portion of the eminent merits of the Lord of the world (Buddha), and therefore I adore and reverence him in worship, but I know not as yet of any religious qualities in these gods of yours that you should desire me to worship them." The Brahmans, hearing these words, with angry scowl began to chide him as a foolish man, and said, "How is it you do not know what divine qualities belong to our gods?" and saying this they forthwith recited the following verses, and said—

> "The city walls of the Asura
> Tower high, with threefold circuit;
> Suspended thus the city hangs in space:
> Full of inhabitants (youths and women).
> Our Deva, bending his bow
> From far, shooting within those city walls,
> Can burn it and destroy it in a moment,
> Like the dry grass burnt up with fire."

Then the Upâsaka having heard these words, with great laughter exclaimed, "According to this I fancy it is of very little account that I do not worship such a being;" and then he replied in a verse as follows—

> "Life is as a drop of dew upon the flower;
> The concourse of all that lives will die.
> Tell me, then, what sign of wisdom is it
> To kill with bow and arrow in addition?"

The Brahmans, having heard these lines, with one voice scolding the Upâsaka, exclaimed, "You are a foolish man! Our Divine Lord, by the power of his heavenly qualities, is able to kill and destroy that wicked Asura, endowed with mighty strength. How say you then he has no wisdom?"

Then the Upâsaka, after their chiding was over, with a deep sigh of sadness added these lines—

> "Distinguish well between the good and bad;
> The wise man, preparing good works,
> Obtains the lasting fruits thereof,
> In future worlds receiving happiness.

But tell me how, in sin and wickedness
Living rebellious, can one acquire religious merit?
Evil purposed, ever-increasing evil,
Flattering himself, 'My evil good accomplishes!'
Because of such seeds of wickedness
Hereafter he shall reap his meed of sorrow."

The Brahmans, having heard these words, first fixed their eyes and raised their hands to heaven, and then furiously shaking their fans at him (or trembling like winnowing fans), addressed the Upâsaka thus: "You are verily a fool and ignorant! Unlucky wretch! not to know that these gods of ours are only deserving of worship, and none others."

Then the Upâsaka, his mind and will unmoved, with gentleness replied, "Although I am alone in this honourable company, yet surely reason does not admit of force (or violence) amongst those who are connected in companionship;" and then the Upâsaka again added these lines, and said—

"The gods you reverence and worship,
Inhumanly and wickedly love to destroy.
But surely, if you sacrifice to these gods,
Considering them deserving of such service,
Then ought you to conceive reverence
Towards the lion, tiger, and wolf,
Who when vexed and angry destroy life.
Evil demons, likewise, and Rakshas,
Foolish men, because of fear,
Ignorantly worship.
But all those who have wisdom
Ought to consider and ponder well.
If towards those who do no harm (cause no pain)
We are naturally drawn with reverence,
Then those are really good
Who cause no harm,
Whilst those who do evil deeds
Cannot but cause harm to others (and so themselves are evil).
If we cannot recognise the good,
Nor separate merit from demerit,
If merit may consist with an evil heart
And demerit with a virtuous mind,

Then murderers and felons
May be well reverenced by the foolish,
And the good and virtuous,
On the other hand, be lightly valued.
Then the world is upside down;
We cannot tell what should be reverenced.
But those born in Gândhâra
Know well how to distinguish the good and bad.
Therefore we believe in Tathāgata,
And pay no regard to Isvaradeva."

When the Brahmans heard these words they rejoined, "Psha! what sort of people come out of Gândhâra, and what religious merit has he you call Buddha?" Then the Upâsaka answered in these words and said—

"Born in the Sâkya palace,
Endowed with all-wisdom,
Dispersing evil as the clouds,
His virtue universally diffused,
Every creature born
From the beginning blessed by him,
Acquainted with the character of all truth,
Thoroughly illuminated,
This great Rishi of ours
We on this account call Buddha."

Then the Brahmans replied in verse and said—

"You call Buddha a great Rishi.
This is a very grievous matter;
For in this Jambudwipa,
The land which Yamarâja holds,
Vasu (or Basa), Basita,
Tai-shih-o-kie-ye (Desâkya?)
Great Rishis like these
Have spread their fame everywhere,
Able to frame (put together) great spiritual charms,
To destroy countries and lands.
You call your Buddha a great Rishi;
He then can make such charms (incantations);

Your famous Buddha also
Should be able to do mighty things:
If he cannot make destructive charms,
How dare you call him a great Rishi?"

At this time the Upâsaka, having no patience at hearing these abusive words, stopped his ears with both his hands, and repeated these gâthas and said—

"Psha! utter not such wicked words,
Such slanderous words as Buddha 'using charms.'
Those who slander the Highest Lord
Shall afterwards receive great affliction."

At this time the Brahmans again replied in verse—

"If Buddha has no manual of charms
He cannot be considered powerful.
If he is a calamity-destroyer,
How can he be a great Rishi?
We only utter true words;
Why speak you then of slander?"

And then the Brahmans, clapping their hands with much glee, said, "Now, then, you foolish fellow, surely you have fallen into a sore dilemma."

At this time the Upâsaka, replying to the Brahmans, said, "Restrain your laughter. You say Tathâgata has no great power and no religious merit. This is false. Tathâgata has indeed great merit and power. He has for ever sapped the root of charmed words, so that they can do no mischief. And now consider well and I will tell you more." Then he said in verse—

"Because of lust and anger and ignorance,
These wicked charms are used;
And when these harmful words are woven,
Then the evil spirits catch the words
And with them hurt the world,
And do deeds of mischief everywhere.
Buddha has cut asunder lust, ignorance, and anger;
His love brings profit and abundance;

Reaching the root of all such charms,
He brings out virtuous deeds in all.
And therefore Buddha, Lord of the world,
Uses no charms to put down evil,
But by the power of his great virtue
Saves us from endless misery.
How then say you Buddha has no great power of purpose?"

Then the Brahmans having heard these verses, their angry mind subsided, and addressing the Upâsaka they said, "We will now ask you a few questions without any anger. Now then, Upâsaka, if Buddha uses no evil charms, why does he not blame those who pay him religious worship? And again, if he cannot do good (by using charms), why is he called a great Rishi?"

The Upâsaka replied, "Tathāgata, the great merciful, in short, uses no evil charms to hurt the world, nor does he only bless because of worship he receives, and for this reason we adore him;" and then he recited the following verses—

"The Great Merciful, who loves all things,
Ever desires to save the world from ill;
Beholding those who suffer,
Their sins upon themselves have brought the ill:
But say not he has used some evil charm,
And so brings evil on the world:
The body of all that lives suffers by nature
In the way of birth, disease, old age, and death,
As the sore resulting from a burning cinder.
How then can he increase the woe?
But rather by his pure and cooling law
He causes all these fiery hurts to heal."

All the Brahmans, hearing these words, immediately hung down their heads, and thought, "These words are good;" and then their hearts tending to belief, they said, "You, Gândhâra, use right distinctions; you seem to believe in things unusual, and therefore you are rightly called Gândhâra—for what is Gândha but 'to hold?'[1]—you hold good principles and let go

[1] Here there seems to be a play on the word Gândharī, the wife of Dhṛitarashtra.

the bad, and so you are rightly named." And then in verse they added this—

"He who is able to hold this earth
He is rightly called 'illustrious friend.'
The first among all 'illustrious friends'
Is truly this 'Gândhâra.'"

Then the Upâsaka thinking, "The hearts of these Brahmans, tending to belief, may yet be made perfect in merit (or in religion). I will now, therefore, further dilate on this subject, and speak of the meritoriousness of Buddha." Then the Upâsaka, with a pleasant countenance, spoke as follows: "I am overjoyed that you have any faith in Buddha; listen, therefore, I pray you, to me for a short time whilst I speak further on this subject of merit and demerit, and do you attend and discriminate." Then he spoke the following verses—

"Consider well the virtues of Buddha,
In every view perfectly complete;
In observing the moral laws, in fixed composure and wisdom,
There is no equal in any respect to Buddha.
Sumeru is the most exalted of mountains,
The ocean is chief amongst flowing streams,
Amongst Devas and men
There is none like Buddha.
Able, for the sake of all that lives,
To undergo every kind of suffering,
So that he might obtain redemption,
And finally not let any perish.
Who is there has sought refuge in Buddha
But has obtained overflowing advantage?
Who is there has taken refuge in Buddha
But has obtained salvation?
Who is there that has followed Buddha's teaching
But has got rid of sorrow?
Buddha by his miraculous power
Has overcome all unbelief (heretics),
His name, therefore, is 'universally spread,'

Filling the universe (the ten regions of space).
Let but Buddha utter his lion voice,
Declare the unreality of all that exists (*sanscâra*),
Speaking without partiality,
Not leaning to either side,
Then both men and gods
Will all repeat 'It is so' (sadhu).
Those who cannot well distinguish the truth
Are still bound in the consequences of their actions.
After the Nirvâna of Tathāgata
Every country made its tower-shrines,
Richly adorned throughout the world,
As the stars hanging in space.
Let every one, therefore, acknowledge
Buddha to be the highest lord."

The Brahmans having heard these words, conceiving faith in their hearts, took the vows of the priesthood and obtained reason.

SERMON II.

Text.

Again, "we must distinguish the true Scriptures from the false. Those who study well what they find in the law will understand this distinction."

I heard in old times that there was a Brahman called Kusika, well acquainted with the Sânkhya Shaster and the treatises of Vyâsa and the Jyotisha Shaster, able to explain and distinguish the points of these and other treatises. This Brahman dwelt in the city Kusumapura (Pâtaliputra). Outside this city there was a village. This Brahman having some business in this village went there, and when arrived he went to the house of a friend. At this time his friend having an engagement had gone out and had not returned. On this the Brahman Kusika addressed one of the household and said, "Have you any book in the house which I can read till the master comes back?" On this the wife of his friend took a book which they had accidentally got, called the Twelve Nidânas, and this she gave to him.

Having got the book, he went to a quiet spot in a grove of trees and began to read it. The book explained how that ignorance (*avidyâ*) caused passion (*sanscâra*), sanscâra caused *vijnâna* (incipient consciousness), from this *nâmarûpa* (rudiments of body, name, and shape), from this the six *âyatanas* (seats of the senses), from this *sparśa* (feeling) [experience of heat and cold, &c.], from this *vedana* (sensation), from this trishna (longing for renewal of pleasurable feeling, and desire to shun that which is painful), from this *upâdâna* (clinging to objects), from this *bhava* (existence), from this birth (*jâti*), from this disease and death. This aggregate of griefs (he read) is called the "great truth of *accumulation*." Ignorance being destroyed, then *sanscâra* is destroyed; *sanscâra* destroyed, then *vijnâna* is destroyed; *vijnâna* destroyed, then *nâmarûpa* is destroyed; *nâmarûpa* destroyed, then the six *âyatanas* are destroyed; these destroyed, then *sparśa* is destroyed; this destroyed, then *vedana* is destroyed; this destroyed, then *bhava* is destroyed; this destroyed, then *upâdâna* is destroyed; this destroyed, then *jâti* is destroyed; this destroyed, then old age, disease and death, sorrow and trouble, pain and loss, the accumulation of pain, all these are destroyed.

When he had read this over once, and did not comprehend it, he then read it a second time, and at once understood the unreality of individual existence. All the systems of the heretics hinge on these two points, that there is an *I* (individuality), and something beyond and distinct from the *I*, but now (he said) I know that all things, born and perishing, have no real principle of endurance. And thinking thus he said, "All other Shastras avoid the question of escaping birth and death, only in this Sûtra have I found the question of escaping birth and death explained."

Then his heart was filled with joy, and raising both his hands, he said, "Now, then, for the first time I have found a true Shastra, I have found now for the first time a true Shastra." And then, sitting gravely as he considered the deep meaning of this principle, his face beamed with delight, as a flower first opening its petals. And then again he said, "Now, then, I begin to understand the way of unloosing the trammels of life and death, and of escaping from mundane existence.

Now I see the folly of all the methods explained by unbelievers, that they are insufficient for escape from birth and death." And rejoicing thus, he said, "Oh, how supremely true is the law of Buddha! how grandly real about cause and result! The cause destroyed, then the fruit is destroyed. The assertions of unbelievers are altogether false and vain which say there is result but no cause for it, not understanding the connection of cause and effect, and therefore knowing no method of escape." Then, thinking of his own former state of ignorance, he felt ashamed, and, smiling, said, "How could I expect to get across the river of birth and death by any such heretical system as that in which I formerly rested? As a man engulfed in the stream of the Ganges whilst bathing is in peril of losing his life, so was it with me when I formerly sought escape from the gulf of birth and death in the way taught by the heretics for in their method there is no way of escape from the world engulfed in the river of birth and death. I was on the point of perishing and my body falling into one of the three evil ways; but now I see in this discourse if I follow the right path I may escape from further birth or death. The words of the Sûtras and Shastras of the heretics are like the words of a fool or a madman; the ninety-six heretical schools are all false and vain; only the way of Buddha is supremely true, is supremely right. The disciples of the six masters, and the rest of the so-called sages, all these saying that they know perfectly all things, are false speakers. Only Buddha, the Lord of the world, is the all-wise; he only is perfectly true, without error."

At this time Kusika repeated the following verses and said—

"The words of the heretical schools
Are false and vain, without reality;
Like the play of a little child
Heaping up the earth to make a city with walls,
The mad elephant treading on it with his foot
Scatters and destroys it so that nothing remains.
Buddha destroys the reasonings of the heretics,
Just the same as in this matter."

Now, then, Kusika the Brahman having conceived the greatest faith in the teaching of Buddha, and heartily reverencing it, cast from him the system of the unbelievers, and rejected all their false speculations, and from morning till evening he pondered and read over the Sûtra of the twelve Nidânas.

And now his kinsman with some Brahmans having returned home, he forthwith asked his wife, saying, "I hear that Kusika has come here; where is he now?" His wife answered her lord and said, "That Brahman having asked me to lend him a book, I gave him one, I know not what it was, and directly he got it, spreading it out[1] with both hands and poring over it, in a moment he cried out with joy, and his appearance has remained ever since like one filled with delight."

Then the husband, hearing these words, went forth to the place where Kusika was, and seeing him gravely seated in meditation, he forthwith questioned him and said, "What is it that now engages your thoughts?" On which Kusika replied in the following verses, and said—

> "Oh, foolish and ignorant,
> Incessantly revolving through the three worlds
> Like the wheel of the potter,
> Whirling round without cessation,
> I am reflecting upon the twelve causes,
> And the way of escape from them."

At this time his kinsman and friend addressed him thus, "Are you able in this book to find any such deep thoughts as these? I got it, indeed, from one of those Sâkya fellows, and I was just going to wash it and erase those words, and use it to copy one of Vyâsa's discourses on." The Brahman Kusika, hearing these words, greatly blamed his relative, and said, "You foolish man! how could you intend to wash out with water the words of this Sûtra? It is an excellent book (Saddharma) of religion; its letters should be written on unalloyed gold and enclosed in a precious casket, and every kind of reverence be paid it;" and then he said these verses—

> "If I had gold and gems,
> And with the gold should build a Stûpa,
> Laying the foundation in the seven precious things,
> Adorning it with gems and hanging curtains,

[1] It is plain from this and what follows that the book was a parchment roll, and was designed to be converted into a palimpsest.

So as to make it exceedingly magnificent,
And if I used it for the worship of this Sûtra—
Though I did all this,
'Twere yet far short of my mind's desire."

Then his kinsman, after hearing these words, becoming impatient, addressed him thus: "What wonderful thing, then, do you find in this religious book (Sûtra) that so far surpasses the writings of Vyâsa that you should wish to do it reverence with gold and all manner of precious stones?"

Then Kusika hearing these words, grieved at heart, and with changed expression of face answered, "Why, then, do you so lightly esteem this Buddhist Sûtra? How can you compare the foolish and extremely vexatious treatises of Vyâsa with these words of Buddha? The writings of Vyâsa know nothing about the distinctions of the law; they confuse cause and effect, and are exceedingly superficial, as in the comparison of the potter (and the clay); and if in these things there is no wisdom to be found in his writings, how much less can we find in them any explanation of cause and effect in relation to man's body and the seats of sensation in that body, and the subject of supreme wisdom?"

Then his friend answered, "If this is as you say, then there is no need of further trouble in speaking on the subject." But the Brahman friends who were present hearing this were grieved, and turning to Kusika they said, "If these words are true, then we cannot nowadays trust in anything Vyâsa says. Is this so?"

Kusika said in reply, "The discourses of Vyâsa are not only nowadays unreliable, but in old times, long ago, those who exercised right discrimination could not long believe in him. And why? In days before the ten-forced (dasabâla) Buddha was born, then all living things were overshadowed with the cloud of ignorance, and, in consequence, were blind and without eyes, and so they thought there was light in these treatises of Vyâsa; but the sun of Buddha having arisen and shed abroad his glorious rays of wisdom, then the words of Vyâsa became obscured and without any meaning, and were fit to be put away, just as the horned owl in the evening comes forth on its wanderings and has strength to exert itself, but when the light comes on, then it hides itself in its covert hole, without strength to serve it. So is it with this Vyâsa; the light of the sun of Buddha having dawned, then his discourses lost their power."

Then his kinsman said, "If it be as you say, and the discourses of Vyâsa cannot compare with the Sûtras of Buddha, then suppose we compare these scriptures with the Sânkhya Shastra."

Kusika said, "The Sânkhya Sûtra says there are five divisions which exhaust the subjects of its discourse, and these five are (1.) authority; (2.) the cause of all; (3.) comparison; (4.) analogy; (5.) certainty; but there is no just comparison in the Sûtra to give light to this argument; for in fact your Sânkhya Sûtra says that Pradhâna alone is not born, a being everywhere diffused and also emanating from every place; but here the Sânkhya Sûtra is at fault, for if Pradhâna is not produced and is substantially present everywhere, if it thus produces everything, it must proceed from some place to use this power of producing, and, therefore, cannot be everywhere substantially present. So that saying there is one thing which creates everything else, and that this one thing is everywhere, is an error. Again, to say that this one thing extending everywhere is able to go from place to place is evidently a contradiction, for if it be everywhere present, where is there for it to go? If it comes and goes, then every place is not everywhere; the two ideas contradict and destroy one another. So that the argument falls through, and it is evidently false to say that anything not produced is able to produce everywhere in all places, able to come, able to go; all this is contradictory."

Then his Brahman friend, having heard these words, spoke to Kusika and said, "It is because you are fraternising with those Sâkya fellows that you speak thus; but in truth in the scriptures of Buddha there are also great errors, for they say that birth and death have no original distinction, and that in the midst of all laws (existence) there is no personality."

Then Kusika, addressing his friend, said, "It is because I find in the scriptures of Buddha the statement that there is no original distinction between life and death, and no personal 'I' (self) in the world, that I believe in him. For if a man speculate about the existence of 'I,' he will find no release in the end. For it is this knowledge of the 'not I' that at once excludes covetous desire, and so produces deliverance; but if a man speculate and assume the existence of 'I,' then there is a place for covetousness and lust; and these being once formulated, then come in life and death, and what escape can there be then?"

On this the kinsman of Kusika addressed him thus: "There is binding, so there is loosing. (There is *sin*, there is *salvation*.) You say there is no 'I,' therefore there is nothing that can be bound and nothing to be loosed. Who, then, is it that obtains deliverance?"

Kusika answered, "Although there is no 'I,' yet there is binding and there is loosing. For why? Because of the over-clouding of sorrow there is a ground for binding. Cut away sorrow, then there is deliverance. So that though there is no 'I,' yet is there something to be bound and something to be released."

On this the Brahmans said, "If there is no 'I,' who is it comes into the next world?"

Then Kusika addressing the men said, "Listen, I pray you. In the past, sorrow wove the net of life, and the body we now have is the result of it; and from the deeds now done will result the body we shall have hereafter, and all its parts. Come, now, I will use a comparison to illustrate this argument. It is like a grain of corn; when all concomitant circumstances are in suitable relation, then the blade is produced; but in truth it is not *this grain* which produces the blade, for the grain dies (in the ground); the new blade grows and increases, but the old grain perishes—because *it* dies *the blade* lives—the two cannot be separated. So it is Buddha speaks with respect to the future body. Although there is no 'I,' yet the fruit of works is not lost."

Then the Brahmans, acquiescing in all that had been said, went forthwith to the priests' quarters, and there asked for permission to take the vows (become "homeless ones"). This having been done, they afterwards became Rahats.[1]

[1] I have omitted some portion of the controversial portion of this Sermon. The whole is very remarkable.

SERMON III.

Text.

Again, "In the religious field we ought not to give preference to either young or old, but regard the character."

I heard an old story of a certain rich patron (Dânapati) who sent a friend of his, a religious man, to a Sanghârama to ask the priests to a repast, but he was only to inquire for the old and important priests, and not to care for the young and inferior. The religious man having asked all the priests in order, then came to the Shamis (novices) and took no notice of them. The Shamis then said, "And why do you not take notice of us Shamis?" In answer he said, "The Dânapati does not require you. It is not my doing." And on remonstrating, the man said these verses—

"The aged possess the merit of years,
White hair and wrinkled countenance,
Bushy eyebrows, teeth falling out,
Rounded shoulders, the limbs cramped.
The Dânapati delights in such,
He cares not about the young."

Now in this temple there was a Shami of distinction who was a Rahat, and as a lion is stirred to anger, so the Shamis provoked him by saying, "That Dânapati is a foolish man; he has no delight in the truly virtuous, but only hankers after the company of the old and infirm." And then they repeated these verses—

"That which is rightly named venerable
Is not necessarily white-haired,
Wrinkled, or with teeth falling out,
For such a person may be foolish and unwise;
But the illustrious man, able to practise a religious life,
Putting away from him and destroying all sin,
Living a pure life of chastity,
This man is rightly called venerable.[1]"

[1] Reverend.

Then all those Shamis immediately, by the power of Irrdhi, changed themselves into shape of aged men; white hair and wrinkled mien, bushy eyebrows, loosened teeth, round-shouldered, leaning on sticks, they went on to the Dânapati's house. The Dânapati having seen them, his heart was filled with joy unspeakable; he burnt his incense, scattered flowers, and quickly asked and forced them to be seated. This done, behold, quite suddenly they all resumed their youthful form as Shamis. Then the Dânapati felt bewildered as he saw the changed appearances, as if by drinking heavenly nectar they had become changed and beautiful so suddenly.

And now the Shami who was a Rahat spoke as follows: "We are not Yakshas or Rakshas, but because you, O Dânapati! have chosen out from the Church the old, thus making a distinction of high and low, and so causing your own good root (*i.e.*, religious principles) to perish, we have caused this transformation to make you repent;" and then he repeated the following verses—

"Just as if the gnat
Desired to exhaust the ocean depths,
So neither can the world fathom
The merit of the priesthood.
The human race could not
By measurement compute its merits;
How much less should you alone
Attempt such calculation!"

Again the Shami continued, "It is wrong to estimate the priesthood by their appearance, whether by age or youth; for the really religious look not at any outward appearance, but only at the presence of wisdom. The body may be young, and yet it may be free from all entanglements and defects, and the possessor of it arrived at the condition of holiness; and though the body may be old, yet the owner of it may be careless and remiss. What you call young and unimportant is not so; and if you think to find the sea of evil desire quite emptied, that is not so; nor yet if you would think to fathom by your wisdom the field of religious merit and know the high and less deserving, can this be done. Have you not rather heard what Tathâgata says in the Sûtra (where he bids his followers) not to despise the little child called 'Snake-fire'? So neither should we despise the young Shamis. And again, what Tathágata says in the Amra comparison, that such fruit may be unripe *within* but ripe in appearance outside, or ripe *outside* and unripe within; so neither is it right to judge men's character by outward appearances. You, therefore, have done very wrong. And now, if you have any doubts upon the matter, you are permitted to ask any question; for hereafter you may have no such opportunity of hearing right distinctions on this point;" and then he continued in verse—

"The sea of the meritorious qualities of the Church
Cannot be fathomed or measured.
In honour of Buddha's birth, in joyful adoration
Arose from space (of themselves) a hundred hymns of praise.
How much more ought incessant praise to sound
On behalf of the great family of man!
Large and vast is the pleasant field of merit;
Sowing little, we reap much.
The accordant Sâkya Congregation,
This is the so-called third precious gem.
Amongst the whole of this assembly
We are not permitted to judge by appearances,
It is not possible to consider any distinction of birth (tribe)
As entitling the possessor to words of commendation.
No one has yet measured his inward excellences;
It is only outward appearance that has produced the respect.
The appearance, indeed, may be young and attractive;
It is wisdom alone that is the recommendation.
Not knowing the inward qualities of heart,
We may esteem a man meanly (who is deserving of much);
As in a thick and bushy grove,
Where grow together the *Tan-peih* and the *I-lan* flowers,
The grove, though full of different shrubs,
Is still so called (*i.e.*, called a *grove*) without distinction of parts;
And so, though there be old and young among the priests,
Yet ought we not to use distinctions.
Kâśyapa, when about to become a recluse,
Taking from his person his very valuable robe,
Assumed the commonest to be found in the vestry,

Valuing it at countless golden pieces
Because of the meritorious character of the priesthood;
So it is in the matter under consideration.
Paying religious offerings to the lowest,
We receive as reward a body endued with tenfold strength.
Just as the waters of the great sea
Will not endure the presence of a dead body,
So is it with the sea of the priesthood;
It will not tolerate a wilful transgressor,
But amongst all the mixed multitude of the priests
Down to the lowest who keeps the first rules (of his ordination),
Honouring this one, and adding religious offerings,
Such an one will secure the reward of great fruit;
Wherefore towards all the priests,
Old and young,
With equal intention, charity should be shown,
And there should arise no distinctions."

At this time the Dânapati, hearing these words, was moved by contrition to such an extent that the hairs of his body stood upright, and his limbs sank under him as he fell to the ground; and as he sought pardon for his fault he exclaimed, "Oh, foolish transgressor that I am! my faults are indeed many. Oh that you would accept my repentance and deign to explain my doubts!" and then he said in verse—

"You indeed possess great wisdom
In dividing the tangled net of doubts.
If I do not ask for explanation,
Then wisdom will not come to me."

At this time the Shami said, "Rest content; what you ask shall be answered." The Dânapati then inquired as follows: "Great sir! which is the more excellent?—to believe and honour Buddha or the Church?"

The Shami answering said, "Do you then not know that there are three Treasures?" (*i.e.*, Buddha, the Law, and the Church).

The Danapati said, "I know indeed that there are three, but

yet, notwithstanding, I wish to know why there may not be amongst the three one greatest?"

The Shami answering said, "There is neither one greater or less than another, whether it be Buddha or the Church;" and then he said these verses—

"The Brahman of a noble family,
Whose name was *Tuh-lo-che* (Varája),
Blaming and praising Buddha in the same breath,
Presented Tathágata with food as a religious offering.
Tathágata declined to receive it;
No one in the three worlds could digest it.
Throwing it straightway into the water,
A steaming vapour rose at the same moment.
Gotamî offering respectfully a robe,
Buddha at once gave it to the priesthood.
Thus he showed by these proceedings
That the three 'Precious ones' are equal and not different."

At this time the Dânapati, having listened to the words spoken, said thus, "With respect to the equality of Buddha and the priesthood, why then did he cast the food on the water and not give it to the priests?"

The Shami answered, "It was to show that Tathágata had no greedy desire for food, and to make the virtuous character of the priesthood manifest, that he so acted; and then Buddha perceiving that such food as this (*i.e.*, offered and so consecrated) no one in the three worlds could partake of, it was therefore he ordered it to be cast into (pure) water, and the fiery vapour at once arose. But with reference to the robe of Gotamî offered to Buddha, he passed it over to the priesthood, and they received it, to show that there is no difference. You should understand this, therefore, that the priesthood is highly honourable (bhadanta), and that the Church and Buddha are equal and the same."

The Dânapati then spoke as follows: "From this time forwards, in honouring the priesthood, whether young or old, I will make no difference, but will offer my gifts with equal aim."

The Shami answered, "If you thus act, ere long you shall obtain the way of seeing truth;" and then he added—

"Much hearing and keeping the precepts,
Dhyána and wisdom,
The man running along the way of the Three Vehicles,
All these bring the same reward.
Like the streams of the Sindhu river,
Flowing onwards, enter the sea,
So these worthy ones and saints
Together enter the sea of the priesthood.
Like as in the midst of the snowy hills
Grow all kinds of medicinal plants,
Or as the good and generous earth
Causes the seeds to grow and increase,
So good and wise men all
Come forth and grow in the field of the Church."

Having recited these gâthas, he further addressed the Dânapati and said, "Have you not at least heard from the Sûtras respecting Aniruddha, Nanda, and Kompira, how that a great spirit-warrior named *Kia-fu* addressed Buddha thus: 'World-honoured! if throughout the worlds a Deva, a man, or Mâra, or Brahma, is able in his mind to recite the names of these three disciples, this shall bring great gain and rest'? But if to name three men does this, how much more the profit accruing from the whole Church?" and then he added in verse—

"Three men, who form but a part of the whole,
Recollecting (naming) them brings profit,
As that spirit-warrior said;
Not able to recite the entire priesthood,
If only these, great gain shall follow.
How much more reciting all the names!
Know this, then, and remember it,
All good and meritorious things
Come from the Church,
Just as the rain from the great Nâga
Can only be absorbed by ocean's depths.
The priesthood is the same;
This only can absorb the great law's rain.
Therefore you ought with single heart
To recite the character of all the Church.
And who are those that make the Church

But the great band of good men,
The body of the converted?
The priesthood, like a valiant host of warriors,
Can overcome and vanquish Mâra the foe.
Thus all this grand fraternity,
This mighty forest invincible in wisdom,
All righteous doers,
Gathered together all in one,
Saved and delivered, surpassing the Three Vehicles.
Oh, what a grand victorious host is this!"

And now the Shami having concluded these laudatory stanzas, the Dânapati and his companions, conceiving great joy of heart, obtained the fruit of Srotâpannas.

SERMON IV.

Text.

Again, "By hearing the law there ensues great profit, and by increase of wisdom the heart is entirely composed and satisfied."

I heard long ago this story about the Lion district (Ceylon). At one time there was a man who procured a Mani gem large as a man's fist. This gem was rare and costly, such as the world could hardly equal. This gem he presented to the king. The king, beholding it when in his possession, said in verse—

"From ancient days the various kings
Collecting gems have sought renown,
And in the midst of tribute-bearers
Have brought their gems to view for their own exaltation.
But when these monarchs come to die,
They have to leave their treasures and depart alone,
With bodies clothed again—no possible escape—
According to their deeds, if good or bad;
Just as the bee that gathers honey—
Another reaps the gain, he gets nothing.
So is it as regards wealth and jewels;
We profit others, nought get ourselves.
From days of old the various kings,
With respect to these deceitful gems,
Have heaped up stones for others' use;

Not one of them to follow him (at death).
Now will I for my own benefit
Cause this gem to follow me.
Only in the merit-field of Buddha
Can future recompense be got."

The king having recited these verses, forthwith went to the place where a Stûpa was built, and caused this jewel to be placed on the top of the surmounting pole. Its brilliancy was equal to that of a large star, so that the king's palace and the adjoining halls were all lit up with its brightness day by day. One day the light suddenly stopped. The king, alarmed on that account, forthwith sent a messenger to see why it was. Having come to the place, he could not see the gem, but only the fallen staff and blood flowing down on the ground. Following the blood traces towards a *Kia-to-lo* wood, on reaching it he found the gem-robber as a rat concealed between some trees. It appeared that whilst he was stealing the gem, the staff broke and fell to the ground, and hence the blood. Immediately seizing the man, he brought him to the king's presence. When the king first saw him he was extremely angry, but observing how he was bleeding and torn, his heart was touched with pity, and looking at him he said, "Psha! man! you are indeed a fool, to steal a gem belonging to Buddha; for if you had succeeded in escaping with it, still hereafter you would have fallen into misery;" and then he said in verse—

"For shame! what folly this!
What want of wisdom doing such wickedness!
As if a man, fearing the stick,
Subjected himself to death and torture,
So, fearful of the pinch of poverty,
You have conceived this wicked scheme;
Not able to endure a moment's want,
You court a long unending wretchedness."

Then a certain minister, having heard these verses, addressed the king and said, "What your majesty says is true and not vain;" and then he added these lines—

"A Stûpa is a precious thing with men;
Who robs a Stûpa, ignorant and foolish,

For countless kalpas he
Shall not meet with the three Precious Ones;
In years gone by there was a man,
Who, for that his heart was full of joy,
Took up a Sumana flower,
And offered it before a Tower of Buddha.
For this, a god or man, through endless kalpas
He enjoyed the highest bliss.
To rob a Stûpa of the Dasabala Lord,
And take its jewels for one's private use,
The fruit of such behaviour certainly
Would show itself engulfed in hell."

Again another minister, angry with the culprit, said, "As this fool of a man has committed such a crime, and it has been proved, he should be tortured (boiled) to death."

The king, answering him, said, "Say not so; for if he were put to death, what more could we do? but having fallen to the ground, we may lift him up again;" and then the king added these verses—

"This man, having fallen so wofully,
We ought with speed to try and rescue him.
I will now give him gold and gems;
Let him repent and get some merit;
Perhaps he may escape (his punishment),
Being on the point of certain misery.
I will give him money;
Let him offer gifts to Buddha,
That as with disobedient heart
He sinned, he may not perish;
For if a man by accident falls down,
He may perhaps be raised again;
For as we sin, 'tis against Buddha,
So he alone can remedy our sin."

Then the king, giving the man money, bade him go offer it to Buddha, and wipe out his guilt and get religious merit.

On which the thief thought thus, "Now, then, if this great king had not been humanised by the religion he professes, he would have caused me to be tortured to death on account of my crime. Now this king is in very truth a great man to counsel me thus in the face of my crime, and Sâkya Tathágata is a wonderful being to be able to convert even an unbeliever thus." Having said this, he went straightway to the Stûpa, and falling on his hands and knees, he adored and said, "Great merciful lord of the world, the true saviour of men! although thou hast reached Nirvâna, yet you can cause your grace to find out me. The world at large calls you its true deliverer; again they name you, 'known and acknowledged everywhere.' Let your favour visit me, for are you not a true deliverer? Oh, let not this name be vain and empty;" and then he said—

"The world names you true saviour;
This name is true, not vain.
Now let this salvation find me out,
Let me know its true significance.
The world is all on fire,
Burnt up with sorrow thick as weeds;
Thy love, cool as the clear moon
Shining abroad, heals every pain.
When Tathágata dwelt in the world,
He saved the wealthy noble
Held in the wilderness by an evil spirit;
This, indeed, was not a hard thing!
But now, after his Nirvâna,
By his bequeathed law to save from misery;
Yea, even me to save from woe!
This is indeed a most hard thing.
What skilful artist he,
Uniting skill with pious heart,
Carved yonder figure, right hand raised,
Which makes the guilty find repose;
The fearful, looking on it,
Feel, as they look, their fears subside.
How much more when in the world
Was he a personal deliverer of many!
Now in my great affliction
His sacred image rescues and delivers me."

SERMON V.

Text.

Again, "The man without desire, though he has riches and worldly goods, his heart not being engrossed by them, he is still called and known as a man without desires."

I heard a story long ago of this kind: There was a certain Upâsaka who had a friend that believed in the way of religion practised by Brahmans. At this time this friend of his was commending a certain Brahman, who, with worn-out clothes, was subjecting himself to endure the broiling of the five fires, eating nothing but vile food, sleeping on dirt; and calling to the Upâsaka, he said, "Will you come with me and see this Brahman? You have never yet seen so greatly mortified a body as his and a man so free from desire; do you know him or not?"

The Upâsaka replied, "How this (man of) exceeding (high) suffering is deceiving you!" and then going with his friend, he spoke to the Brahman thus, "What are you expecting to result from your mortification?"

The Brahman said, "I am enduring these torments with a view to becoming a king."

At this time the Upâsaka spoke to his friend and said, "This man, as it now appears, is seeking to obtain the treasures of the great earth, the jewels and gold, the killing and eating, palace servants, music and women, and every kind of pleasing entertainment; he is not contented with the wealth or the treasures of a minister or a nobleman, but he must needs have the jewels and treasures of the great earth. How can you call this man one of no desire? You can only see the man's body that suffers torment, and on that account you call him a man of 'few desires,' but you cannot, in knowledge of his insatiate purpose, call him a man of small desire." And then he spoke these verses—

> "He who is called a man of small desire
> Need not be badly clothed or fed,
> Or without the means of life's enjoyments,

So as to be thought of small desire.
For this man here before us,
His mind is like the great ocean-river :
He covets more than he can tell.
How can such a man have small desires ?
He undergoes these painful sufferings
Because he covets thoroughly the indulgence of the
five desires.
This man is false and hypocritical ;
He only shows the outward marks of small desire ;
Because he covets much he suffers pain ;
This is a false pretence to small desires."

Having recited these verses, the Upâsaka said again, "This man is full of covetous desire, anger, and delusion ; he has no share at all with those Rishi saints who suffered discipline. You ought to know that men of small desires are not always poor. They may be rich and possessed of every kind of treasure, and yet be truly men of small desire. For instance, Bimbasâra Râja was rich, possessed of lands and elephants, horses, and the seven kinds of gems, and he was rightly called a man of small desires. And why? Because, though he had wealth and treasure, still his heart was free from covetousness, and he rejoiced in holiness ; and therefore though so rich and possessed of every treasure, yet because his heart was free from longing, he was truly one of small desire. And so again, although a man possesses nothing, no wealth or jewels, yet if he have an insatiate longing, he cannot justly be called a man of small desire ;" and then again he said in verse—

"If, without food or clothing,
Your naked Nirgranthas and the rest
Subject themselves to every torment
In order to secure the name of Saint,
Starved ghosts and cattle,
Paupers, and those in tribulation—
These, and all who suffer from calamity,
Would also rightly so be called,
As much as those.
Self-inflicted torture,
May cause the body pain,

But yet the heart may cherish covetous desire
And long for unbounded gain :
That man cannot be called 'of small desire.'
And so, again, a man possessing all things,
His heart polluted not with longing,
But practising the love of holiness,
He is rightly called 'of small desire.'
Just as the ploughman
Sows in his field all kinds of seed,
But covets more when the grain ripens,
He is not called a man 'of small desire;'
But he who regards the body as some evil sore
That must be tended with all necessary care,
Because he seeks through it to get true wisdom,
This man is one 'of small desire.'
He tends the soul to cure it,
But has little thought about indulgences.
The heart desiring nothing except this,
This man, in truth, is one of 'small desire.'
His mind's intention not being crooked,
Not seeking personal fame or profit,
Although he has provision for his comfort,
Yet being true, and well reputed,
Who acts and lives like this,
He is indeed a man 'of small desire.'"

Sermon VI.

Text.

Again, "Although a man keep the precepts, if he does so with a view to obtain heavenly delights (or the pleasures of heaven), he does but break the precepts."

I have heard an old story of this kind. There was a Shaman who dwelt in a certain deserted wood, observing the summer rest with a certain Brahman. On this occasion the Shaman kept continually going forward and backward past the place where the Brahman was, but in his behaviour to him he was neither too familiar nor too distant, but tried to observe the just medium. And why? because undue familiarity would have bred rudeness, and too distant a line of conduct would have produced hatred. And he recited the following verses—

"Place a stick in the sunlight,
If it slope to one side, there will be no right shadow;
But fix it perfectly upright
And the shadow then will be of proper length.
With this man it is the same;
A right medium between familiarity and distance
Will lead to a gradual acquaintance,
And after this I may instruct him in religion."

"This Brahman (he said) is without true wisdom; he distinguishes not between the offerings of the foolish or the worthy; his extreme suffering is the cause thereof. I will neither be familiar nor distant with him, for this very inability through suffering to take notice of the offerings of others is in itself a suffering;" and so gradually, by use of means, getting into conversation with him, he put this question, "Why are you now lifting up your hands towards the sun, sleeping on ashes, or sitting naked as you are now on the grass, or not sleeping day or night but standing with one foot raised? What is it you are trying to get by all these austerities?"

The Brahman answered, "I seek to get a kingdom and to govern it as king."

A short time afterwards this Brahman fell sick, and on going to get a doctor's prescription, he was told by the physician that he must get some meat to eat. On this the Brahman spoke to the Bhikshu and said, "Can you go for me to the house of the Dânapati and beg a morsel of meat to heal my sickness?"

Then the Bhikshu thought thus with himself, "If I am to convert that man, now is my opportunity."

Having thought thus, he caused to appear a sheep, which he brought, led by a tether, to the Brahman.

On the Brahman asking where the piece of flesh was that he wanted, the Bhikshu replied, "This sheep is the flesh." Then the Brahman, greatly enraged, answered, "Would you have me kill the sheep to get the flesh to eat?" On this the Bhikshu answered thus in verse—

"Now you profess to pity a sheep,
And declare you would not kill it,
But hereafter, if you become a king,
Both oxen, sheep, and pigs,
With fowls and wild creatures,
You will slay innumerable.
Then you will sit upon your throne.
And your attendants serving you with food
Will, if you by chance get angry,
Be forthwith decapitated;
Or you will say, 'Cut off their hands and feet,'
Or at another time you'll say, 'Bore out their eyes.'
But now, forsooth! you pity a sheep,
But then you'll readily kill many things.
If really you profess a pitiful heart,
Then you'll forego this thought of royalty;
For as a man about to undergo the torture,
Fearing the pain, will drink much wine
[And so delude himself],
Or as the flowery grove is very brilliant
Which is about to be consumed with fire;
Or as a fetter made of gold,
Though beautiful, is strong to bind,
So is a king's estate.
Filled with fear and anxious doubtings,
He goes surrounded by his armed attendants,
Glittering with jewels:
He sees not the calamity about to happen.
The foolish crowd, coveting such rank,
Obtaining it, rush into wickedness,
And then fall down to hell (three ways);
Just as the moth loves the fire-glare,
And rushing to the flame is burnt to death.
But though men get the pleasure of the five indulgences,
And though their fame be everywhere diffused,
They only reap incessant fear
And sorrow's anguish deep as possible,
Like treading on a poisonous snake,
Or holding a burning torch before the wind,
Or as one confined within a murderer's house,
Or as one just going to execution.

A king, on going abroad,
Wears his royal crown upon his head,
Glittering with gems and gold;
His royal apparel shines with richness,
His horse or costly chariot
Carries him, as forth he goes
With thousands attending him,
Full of dignity and strength.
But now a hostile band of robbers,
At sight of him so richly dressed,
Attack: if conquered, many slain!
If defeated he, then lost his life!
'Tis true his body is perfumed with richest scents,
His clothes exhale delicious odours,
His food is rare and rich in quality,
A hundred dainty tastes delight his palate,
Whate'er he wants is ready at his word,
There's none to oppose or contradict his will;
Yet, going or coming, sitting or sleeping,
His mind is moved by doubt or lurking fear:
He trusts not friends or relatives;
His very kith and kin
Are ever plotting evil.
What pleasure can there be in such a state?
'Tis like the fish that nibbles at the hook,
Or like the honey covering up the knife,
Or like the net or baited trap;
The fishes or the beasts desire to taste,
But see not their impending suffering.
The case is so with wealthy folk,
Who now enjoy their luxuries, but in the end are born in hell.
In hell, whose very walls
And every corner, nay, the very earth, is molten fire.
The sinner there lies writhing;
The fire bursts from out his body
While he receives unmitigated torments.
Consider, then, and weigh the matter.
The joys to be partaken of, how few!
The pain and suffering, how great!
Ponder well and recollect the pain,

And seek not rank or independence;
Let go your grasping covetous mind,
And seek to find entire escape,
Pain's final and complete destruction."

The Brahman, having heard these verses, remained silent without answering; but then, with joined hands, turning to the Bhikshu, he said, "Honoured sir! you are skilled in opening the understanding. My mind indeed was set on getting the royal state in the thirty-three heavens, and I cared nothing for eternal life (sweet dew);" and then he repeated these gâthas—

"Illustrious art thou in devising means,
Thy wisdom is able to discriminate justly.
For my sake destroying in me false aims,
Leading me on in the right road,
A true friend indeed is this.
Praised and honoured in the world,
May such a friend be ever mine
Without the pain of cavil or dispute,
Leading my mind's thoughts in the true way
Out of error into the right path of religion,
Showing me the works of virtue and of vice,
Causing me to attain salvation."

Sermon XX.[1]

The Text.

Once more, "To give away in charity (our possessions), without any change of purpose, is the way to secure high renown in the present world and a full reward (hereafter): we ought therefore to be liberal and not niggardly."

I have heard that once on a time there was a certain painter (decorator) belonging to the country of Bactria (*Fu-kie-lo*), whose name was *Kie-na* (Kana?), who had some business to transact at Takshasila. Having arrived there, he visited all the Stûpas (Stûpa temples), and having decorated a certain vihâra, he received in return for his work thirty gold pieces.

[1] I translate this short Sermon because it shows us that the Vihâras in India were decorated by artists from Bactria (where Greek art prevailed) at an early period. It also shows us that Buddhism and Buddhist worship prevailed in Bactria at the same time.

Having returned to his own country, he found all the people engaged in celebrating a five-yearly assembly (*panchavarsha parishat*).

Having been brought to a state of faith (by what he witnessed), he asked the Bhikshu who was managing the affairs, who was going to provide the necessary entertainment (food, &c.) for the morrow? In reply he said that no one had come forward to offer his services.

He then inquired of the same Bhikshu how much one day's entertainment (for food, &c.) would cost; and hearing that it would take thirty gold pieces, the painter immediately gave to the Bhikshu that sum, his own earnings at Takshasila. He then went home.

And now his wife inquired of him, "What have you earned whilst on your travels abroad?" The husband answered, "I got thirty gold pieces, but I have given them away in charity to the religious assembly."

His wife, having heard this, was very angry, and sent to call all their relations, and addressed them thus: "This husband of mine, after he had got some gold pieces by his work abroad, has given it all away in charity to the assembly, and now there is nothing left for our domestic expenses."

Then all the relations, seizing the man, took him to the magistrate's office and said, "It cannot be allowed that this man, who is of poor estate, should not employ the earnings of his craft in supporting his family, but, in spite of his relations' means being exhausted, should give away (what he has earned) in charity (to entertain) the religious assembly."

The magistrate having heard the complaint, asked the man, "Is this the case with you or not?" He answered, "It is all true." At this time the magistrate, having listened to the statement and answer, was deeply moved, and immediately spoke as follows in commendation of the man's conduct: "Well done!" And then having taken off his robes and all his jewels and saddled his horse, he placed the man thus clothed on the steed and repeated the following lines—

"How difficult for one enduring the pain of poverty,
Who has by his hard labour earned some scanty reward,

To bestow it in charity (for some religious purpose),
And not employ it for purposes of daily life!
Even though a man be rich and possess abundance,
Though his means of livelihood increase exceedingly,
Yet, unless he use due consideration and thought,
He is not quickly led to devote any portion of it in charity;
But if, by consideration of his after state,
He brings himself to feel that charity meets with its due reward,
And then with determination sets himself to charitable acts,
Banishing all niggard and miserly inclinations,
This man thus practising his religious duties
Shall escape from the destruction which the *earth-holder* brings on the world."[1]

At this time the painter, having heard the verses, was filled with joy, and exultingly he advanced, riding on the caparisoned horse and clothed in the robes (of the magistrate), towards his home. Then the members of his household, seeing one so gorgeously attired riding a horse and coming to the gate, exclaimed, "Here comes a great personage!" and their hearts failing them for fear, they ran indoors and hid themselves from sight. On this the painter addressed them and said, "I am no stranger, but your husband and master." The wife then addressed him thus, "You are a poor man, how then have you got this caparisoned horse to ride and these clothes?" Then the master repeated these lines—

"Listen and attend, good wife!
Whilst I recite a true tale.
Money given in religious charity,
This charity, though not yet producing fruit,
Is but like the seed sown in the earth,
Which at first seems lost, but then shoots up.
The field of religious merit is good beyond description;
The fruit it produces comes afterwards.
In this good field of priestly charity
Who would not wish to sow?
When once the mind is so made up,
Then all shall see the fruit produced."

[1] Perhaps the same as *Yama*.

Then the good wife, after listening, arrived at a pure and believing heart, and replied in these verses—

> "Even as Buddha declares,
> Religious charity is exceedingly productive.
> He who now gives in charity
> Shall surely reap where he has bestowed;
> For whosoever piously gives a little water,
> He shall receive return like the great sea.
> Amongst all human associations
> The priesthood of Buddha is the chief.
> At time of death, wherever points the thought,
> The flower as it opens stands (or *goes*) before."

[This last stanza seems to refer to the old idea that each dying saint is represented by a flower opening in Paradise.]

I will conclude by calling your notice to some remarks made by *I-tsing* in the 32nd section of his work, "*Nan-hae-k'i-kwei-ch'un,*" as to the character of the hymns used in Buddhist worship, some of which were composed by Aśvaghosha.

The land of China, he says, from ancient times, according to traditional teaching, has only known the worship of Buddha by setting forth his names. But in the Western countries the Chaityas which stand by the roadside are reverenced by passers-by. And every afternoon or evening the assembly coming from the gates (by the convent) three times circumambulate the Stûpas with incense and flowers; and then sitting down cross-legged, they cause some skilled brother to accompany himself with music as he sings with clear voice the praises of the Great Master; and for this purpose they have hymns consisting of ten or even twenty ślokas. They then return to the temple, and having taken their seats in the usual place, they cause a preacher to mount the pulpit (lion-seat), and there to read through some short sermon (Sûtra). The pulpit is not far from the chief Sthavira's seat, and is not so high or so large. In reading the Sûtra (or whilst reading), they generally recite (sing) from the Sangita (or *threefold collection* [1])

[1] This expression is afterwards explained to refer to the three *sections* or *divisions* of the compilation which Aśvaghosha made. It may have been in the form of a *triptych*.

(*San-k'he*) which Aśvaghosha Ayusmat compiled, selecting ten ślokas or so, and as they catch the meaning of what is read, they recite the hymn of praise [1] to the three honoured names; (the preacher then) sets forth the place where the several passages occur in the true Sûtra spoken by Ananda.[2] The hymn or psalm being ended, they then select ten other ślokas to recite whilst they perform the usual votive procession (round the apse [3] [*hwui hiang*]). This is also composed in three parts or sections, and hence it is called *San-k'he*. All this being ended, the congregation says "*Svasti*" (Be it even so) [AMEN]; this is a very favourite or choice exclamation of assent used during the recitation of the Scriptures. They also say "Vatthu," which is the same as "It is well" (*saddhu*). The preacher after this descends (from his pulpit). The president then first rises and bows to the lion-throne (the pulpit), (in token of) the preparatory instruction (or, the service) being finished, and afterwards he bows to the holy assembly, and then returns to his place. The second priest then bows to the two places (viz., the pulpit and the assembly), and then salutes the president, and then resumes his seat. The third priest then does likewise, and so on to the end of the assembled priests. If the number of priests is very great, then three or five, as they think proper, rise at the same time and salute as before. This done, they depart.

This is the rule of the priesthood throughout the holy land of the East from Tamralepti to Nalanda. In the latter monastery the number of priests and disciples is so great, amounting to about five thousand, that such an assembly in one place would be difficult. This great temple has eight halls, each able to hold about three hundred at a time; in these the various congregations are assembled. The rules here are (in consequence of the numbers) somewhat different from other places. They

[1] Probably the *Sarandgamana*, or "glorious hymn," as Buddhaghosha terms it, in honour of the Buddha, the Law, and the Church. *Vide* Childers, J.R.A.S., vol. iv. part ii. p. 325.

[2] So at least I understand the expression *Fo-ts'in*.

[3] The Chinese expression *hwui-hiang* exactly corresponds to the Greek ἄψ or ἄψ ἰέναι. The last portion of the Buddhist ritual in worship consists of a processional circuit round the spot where, in old times, the *dágaba* or relic shrine stood, viz., in the chord of the apse. I am not suggesting that the word *apse* is derived from ἄψ, but simply pointing out the coincidence.

select one singing-master (precentor), who, every evening towards sundown, goes through the various halls where the priests are assembled accompanied by a *pure brother*,[1] a young man [acolyte], who precedes him, holding flowers and incense; and as they pass through the assemblies the members of the congregation bow down, and at each bow with a loud voice they chant a hymn of three ślokas or five, with the sound of drums and music. At sundown, when all is just over, the precentor receives from the temple property a certain allowance as an offering (offertory), after which he again takes his place opposite an incense-heap (a large censer), and singly recites with his heart (or heartily) a hymn of praise; and thus until nightfall, when, after the congregation have given three complete prostrations, the assembly is broken up. This is the traditional custom of worship in the West. The old and sick occupy small seats apart.

There were some ancient practices not exactly the same as the present Indian customs; such, for instance, as the custom of chanting a hymn when at the time of worship the distinctive marks of Buddha were recited; this was a grand chant of ten or twenty ślokas: this was the rule. Again, the "Gâthas of the Tathágatas" and others were originally intended to be laudatory hymns in praise of the virtues of Buddha, and were in long or short verses arranged harmoniously. And because the meaning of these verses was difficult to be got at, it became customary during the religious seasons, when the congregation was assembled in the evening, to call on some distinguished member to recite 150 to 400 stanzas in praise of Buddha (and explain them), with other hymns.

There have been certain leading men of great talent who have contributed hymns of praise for use in the worship of Buddha—such as venerable *Mātrijāta*, a man of great talent. Of him it is said that his birth was predicted by Buddha when a certain parrot saluted him as he passed through a grove. Having become a convert, he first composed 400 laudatory verses and afterwards 150, arranged according to the six para-

[1] A similar expression is used by *Fă-hien* (cap. 3). The Essenes also had *pure brothers* to wait on them.

mitas, illustrating the most excellent qualities of the world-honoured Buddha.

Other hymns were composed by the Bodhisatwa Asangha, others by Vasabhanda. All who enter the ministry are supposed to learn these beforehand, whether they belong to the Great or Little Vehicle. There are also the hymns composed by Channa Bodhisatwa, by Sakyadeva of the Deer Park, and also by Nagarjuna, who composed the work called *Sukrita.* This he left to his old patron, the king of a great southern kingdom called Sadvaha.

We cannot pass over the special notice of the *Jâtakamala,* which is also a book of this sort. If translated it would make about ten chapters in Chinese. The origin of the book was this: Silâditya[1] Râja was extremely fond of literature, and on one occasion issued an order that all the chief men of the kingdom who loved poetry should assemble the next day morning at the palace, and each bring a verse on paper. In consequence five hundred assembled, and on their papers being opened the verses were put together, and this is the Jâtakamala.[2] Of all books of poetry known in India, this is the most refined. The islands of the Southern Sea and the ten countries all use these verses, but in China they have not yet been translated.

Again, the venerable Aśvaghosha composed a book of chants, and also the Alaṁkâra Shastra, and also the Life of Buddha in verse. The whole book if translated might be included in about ten volumes. It describes the life of Tathágata from the period of his birth in the palace, to his death between the trees. This is used also throughout India and in the Southern Sea.

---

[1] Siláditya died 550 A.D. Jul. i. 215.

[2] This may be the copy of the *Jâtakamala* alluded to lately by Dr. Frankfurter (I think) in the *Athenæum.*

LECTURE IV.

COINCIDENCES BETWEEN BUDDHISM AND OTHER RELIGIOUS SYSTEMS.

IT is curious that whilst Xenophanes, the founder of the Eleatic School in Greece, was being led "purely by his own reflections to the profoundest doubts concerning the religion of the people," that a similar process of thought was taking place in the mind of the founder of Buddhism in India. Both these reformers were dissatisfied with the popular form of belief, and purely by their own reflections were led to one conclusion. The Grecian philosopher declared "that there could be but one God, the highest among gods and men, who is all eye and all thought, and who without effort rules all by the insight of his mind." Buddha announced himself to be "the highest among gods and men, who had attained supreme wisdom, and was possessed of an all-seeing eye (*Samanta chaksu*)."

In the former case, the objective belief in God remained intact; in the latter, the belief in God was identified with the consciousness of an indwelling enlightenment, attained by the removal of that which prevented its manifestation, by a process which had continued through ages of discipline.

The movement adverse to the popular belief, as in Greece so in India, had been going on for many years before the time either of Xenophanes or Buddha.

In Greece it had been aided by the expressed sentiments of a succession of poets and philosophers, Solon, Pindar, Æschylus, Sophocles, Socrates, and others; in India there had been a succession of mystic philosophers from the time of the Vedas (corresponding to the Homeric period in Greece) down to the time when Buddha appeared, who had each attempted to attenuate, so to speak, the gross naturalism of the popular worship, by the invention of heaven above heaven, each less sensuous than the one underlying it, placed in order through successive tiers, till at last they had well-nigh done away with the possibility of any local character for the heavens they invented, or any conceivable existence for those who inhabited them.

The difference between the movement in India and Greece was this—in the former country we see before us, in the very names of the heavens invented, the stages of thought that succeeded one another in successive periods of advance; in the latter, the process was unmarked by any such steps, but was a purely intellectual one.

We read that Buddha, when he left his home, hoping to solve the question of "the existence of sorrow," held parley with certain ascetic philosophers who were reputed to be in advance of the age with respect to the solution of this question. Arāda and Udra Râmaputra had framed for themselves an idea of future life in which the existence of sorrow should be impossible, because they did away with any subject capable of it. They imagined a state of existence "without form" and "without thought;" this conception, however, did not satisfy the young prince, because there was still an individual existence, and therefore a possibility of re-birth in a lower form of life, and therefore of continued suffering. Buddha, therefore, sought out for himself the answer to his own question, "What is that condition in which renewed birth and death is impossible?"

He found this in his theory of Nirvâna. Among other terms used in explanation of this expression in Chinese Buddhist works is the one I referred to in my First Lecture, viz., the term *wou-wei.* In the thirtieth section of the *Fo-pen-hing-king* the phrase is used *Tan-wou-wei,* "praises of Nirvâna." *Wou-wei,* whether it mean non-action or non-individuality, seems to point to "a breathless" or "non-creative" state of existence. When *desire* sprang up in this condition, then sorrow began. This desire led to production, and production is necessarily evil. Go back, therefore, "stem the flood," Buddha taught, destroy the root of desire, and you will arrive at a condition of original perfection. Whether the term Nirvâna may not be explained etymologically as signifying a condition of "*not breathing forth,*" *i.e.*, passive and self-possessed existence, is a question I shall not attempt to answer. But on one point there is agreement in all Buddhist works that have come before me, that Nirvâna is a condition incapable of beginning or ending (without birth, without death).[1] This conception developed finally into the worship of the eternal (*Amitâyus*), a worship still professed (though ignorantly) wherever this development has been allowed to progress on the lines of Buddha's original thought.

There is an expression found in the Chinese as a synonym for the name of Buddha, I mean "*Chin Yu*" (the "true *that*," or, *thus*), which evidently points in the same direction. "The true That" is the state of existence, ineffable and unthinkable, to which the Buddha has returned. I need not remind you how this idea of non-breathing existence (*i.e.*, passive and non-creative being) is exhibited in the direct efforts both of Buddhists and Brahmans to suppress their breath when in a state of profound religious thought or ecstasy, as indicating a brief return to the condition of perfect and unfettered being. And, in fact, the modes of thought and expression on this particular point (indicating agreement derived probably from a primitive origin), common both to Semitic and Aryan, and probably Turanian nations, is very remarkable. The act of creation is attributed in Semitic records to the "breath or Spirit of God moving upon the waters." If it be remembered that the "Spirit of God" may justly be rendered "a mighty wind" (although from *our* standpoint there is no need to adopt such a rendering), this offers a remarkable agreement with the "strong wind blowing on the waters" explained in Buddhist records, which I shall presently translate as the origin of the created world.

The condition of "*non-breathing*" or "not blowing," then, is the same as a condition of passive or non-creative existence, which is supposed to have been the original state of *that*, ere desire arose and multiplicity ensued. It is to this condition Buddha aimed to return when he taught us to extinguish desire, and so reach Nirvâna.

But whilst we may regard Buddhism in the light of a reformation of the popular belief in India, we must bear in mind that the stream of tradition, which reappears in its

[1] Corresponding to the Egyptian description of Kneph, "*τὸ ἀγγένητον κὰι τό ἀθανὰτον.*"

teaching and may be traced in its books, is independent and probably distinct from the Brahmanical traditions embodied in the Purânas and elsewhere. At any rate, this is the case so far as the primitive questions of creation and of the kosmic system generally are concerned. Mr. Rhys Davids[1] has already remarked "that the Buddhist archangel or god Brahmâ is different from anything known to the Brahmans, and is part of an entirely different system of thought." I am inclined to go further than this, and say that the traditions of the Buddhists are different from those of the Brahmans in almost every respect.

First of all, it is singular that the Buddhists, by a sort of *à priori* reasoning, should have arrived at the truth of an infinite number of worlds existing throughout space. "Worlds as numerous as the sands of the Ganges," is a phrase entirely their own; and by a higher enumeration, "worlds as many as all the sands of all the Ganges rivers;" till at last they formulated the expression "worlds innumerable" (*asaṁkheya*). By an equally singular process of thought they conceived the existence of a universally diffused vital or organic force, which they called *Bodhi*, or, to use the words of M. Leon Féer,[2] "Au principe de l'impuissance de l'instabilité universelle il (*Bouddha*) oppose l'existence d'une force réelle la seule chose qui subsiste, la Bodhi." It is into this *force* those who are enlightened (the Buddhas) pass when they die. And by this force all things are sustained and upheld. Hence the "heart of Bodhi" is a frequent term, used to indicate the power or the presence of this *force* in the heart, which in the later Buddhist speculation constitutes a Bodhisatwa.

Both these deductions are purely Buddhistic and very singular, as they anticipated what is now recognised as scientifically true.

But let us look at the Buddhist kosmic system. This system postulates first of all the existence of a single world, which consists of a central mountain, Sumeru or Meru, round which there are a succession of rocky circles; beyond the seventh of these circles is the great salt ocean, in which this earth of ours, divided into four quarters, is placed; beyond the ocean is a wall

---

[1] Buddhist Suttas, p. 168 n.

[2] Etudes Buddhiques, p. 78.

of iron that embraces the whole; above the central mountain are a succession of heavenly abodes or mansions (*bhuvanas*). The multiplication of these worlds and systems of worlds led to the idea of an infinity of systems, to which I have alluded. The definition of Sumeru or Sumé in Buddhist works is "a mountain of wonderful height;" it is also explained as a mountain of "good light."[1] It is plain that this idea of a lofty central primeval mountain belonged to the undivided human race. It is the *Harô Berezaiti*, or rather the *heart* (*zaredhô*) of these mountains, represented by Alborz[2] of the present day: *barez* or *baresh* (Ved. *bṛihas*) also means *high*. So again we are told that "light rises up from Hara Berezaiti (Alborz);"[3] here we have the other idea, conveyed in the Chinese description of Sumeru—the mountain of "good light." It is on this mountain, again, that "the abode of the gods rests," according to the Zendavesta,[4] and so, also, as we shall see, the Buddhists place the abodes of their thirty-three gods on Sumeru. But in the case of Alborz it would seem as if it was a *rest* or *support* of the heavenly abodes, for so we read in Fargard xix.,[5] "She makes the soul of the righteous one go *above* the Hara Berezaiti; above the *K*inva*d* bridge she places it in the presence of the heavenly gods themselves." Here the idea is that the gods reside above this mountain, which is, as it were, the *support* of their dwellings. This brings to our mind the fable of Atlas supporting the heavens; the same idea may probably be traced in the Greek "Olympus" (Sans. *âlamba*, a support).[6]

This idea of "height" applying to the mountain that supports heaven may in the first instance have referred to the heavens themselves. In the "Odyssey," and in Sophocles also, the idea of Olympus has become generalised or idealised "to the conception of an exalted divine region, and approximates near to that of οὐρανὸς, so that οὐρανὸς and ὄλυμπος interchange synonymously;"[7] and again the same writer says, "There is nothing in

[1] *Vide, inter alia*, Eitel, Handbook, *sub voc.*
[2] Haug, Parsis, 216 n.
[3] Zendavesta, by Darmesteter, 225 n.
[4] Op. cit., 213 n.
[5] Op. cit., 213 (30, 98).
[6] The old lexicographers, singularly enough, define ὄλυμπος from ὁλόλαμπος, "the altogether shining," which corresponds with the explanation given above of Sumeru and Alborz.
[7] Geddes, p. 262.

the 'Odyssey' which obliges us to think of the *Mount* Olympus;"[1] and Professor Campbell remarks, "Olympus, the seat of the gods, is in Sophocles a sort of unseen heaven, and has almost lost the association of *place*." This worship of *height* in the abstract is illustrated in a singular way by a consideration of the origin of a Chinese symbol signifying "the heart" (or more properly the "âtman," or "universal self" of the Brahmans). This symbol is composed of the moon's crescent and three stars or points (*tim*) above it, and is pronounced "săm" or "sim" (*Edkins*). It corresponds with the *chandra vindu* in Sanscrit, and has a somewhat similar sound. Now this symbol of the moon's crescent with the dots above it is a primitive one, to denote that "which is highest,"—the sun, moon, and stars being the regular ascending grade for the heavens. If, then, we may refer the old Chinese sound "*săm*" to that which is the highest, there is no reason why this should not have been a primitive root, and denoting height, have been afterwards referred to the highest mountain round which the primitive race of man congregated. At any rate, in the Buddhist records the mountain is spoken of as *Sumé*, the *high* and resplendent. Whether the Latin *summus* may be related to the same root is a question for further consideration.[2]

In any case, the idea of *height* enters into the Semitic term for heaven, and so we read in Goldziher,[3] "The idea of height in the Semitic religion, as applied to heaven, is shown in the root *sâma* and *râm*, both of which express the idea of being *high*."

Be this as it may; the Buddhist tradition makes the flowings of ocean (the salt ocean) to surround the earth, which is divided into four large islands or quarters. To the south of Sumeru they place the island called Jambu or Jambudwipa. This is described as the "land of excellent gold."[4] We are here reminded of the land of Havilah, "where there is gold, and the gold of that land is good." Another tradition[5] is to the effect that there is a great tree in this land underneath which is "excellent gold,"

[1] Page 263.
[2] The prefix *su*, however, in Sumé is generally regarded as a distinct particle, as εὖ in Greek.
[3] Page 71.
[4] Catena, p. 35 n.
[5] Hi-shi-king, "Book of Genesis" (origin of the world).

and from the name of this tree the land derives its name. With reference to this land of Jambudwipa,[1] the Buddhists say that in the midst of it is a centre (heart), called the lake *A-nieou-to* (Anavataptu); it lies to the south of the Fragrant Mountains and to the north of the great Snowy Mountains (Himavat). It is 800 li in circuit.[2] In the midst of this lake is the abode of a Nâga, who is, in fact, only the transformed appearance of Dasabhumi Bodhisatwa (or of the Bodhisatwas of the ten earths). From his dwelling proceed four refreshing rivers, which compass Jambudwipa. At the east side of the lake, from the mouth of a silver ox, flows out the Ganges river. After compassing the lake once, it enters the sea towards the south-east. From the south side of the lake, from the mouth of a golden elephant, flows the Sindhu river. After compassing the lake once, it enters the sea on the south-west. On the west side of the lake, flowing from the mouth of a horse of lapis-lazuli (vaidûrya), flows the river Foh-tsu (Vakshu, *i.e.*, Oxus), which, after compassing the lake once, enters the sea on the north-west. On the north side of the lake, flowing from the mouth of a pó-chi (sphâṭika, crystal) lion, flows the river Sidâ,[3] which, after making one circuit, flows into the sea on the north-east.[4]

We seem to have in this account a form of the ancient tradition respecting the four rivers flowing out of Eden or paradise; for we can hardly doubt that the mountain from which these rivers flowed was a later form of the Sumeru myth, and on the top of Sumeru is placed the paradise of the thirty-three gods. I will give a brief description of this paradise. It is situated on the central plateau of the mountain. In the middle is the golden city. This city has five hundred gates. Within the city are streets and palaces. Outside the city are beautiful parks. The abodes of the minor gods (Devas) are in the neighbour-

---

[1] "Si-yu-chi," quoted by Jinchau, p. 4.

[2] Quoting from the "Hi-shi-king," Jinchau says, "At the top of the Snowy Mountains, composed of all precious substances, there are four golden peaks, and in the centre one very high peak (ἀκροτάτη κόρυφη), in which there is a Dragon Lake, fifty yojanas round."

[3] Concerning this river, *vide* Minayef, "Grammaire Palie," pp. viii., ix.

[4] This is the origin of the Yellow river; for the *Sidâ*, after flowing underground, comes out beneath the Tsih rocks (on the western frontier of China), and gives rise to the Hoang-ho.—*Ch. Ed.*

hood of these parks. These abodes are surrounded by walls, railings, and tinkling curtains and trees. On the north-east side of the city, but outside of it, is the Tree of Life [*Un-shing*, perfect life]. (The *pârijâta* tree of later Brahmanism.) There is a Yaksha spirit, called Vajrâpaṇi (strong, or diamond hand), who keeps guard in the middle of the city, and five hundred who keep guard at each gate. We have in this description an instance of the *pairi-daêza* of the Zendavesta, a "circumvallation" or "enclosure."

With respect to the creation of the world and the heavens, the Buddhist legend is that there are periods (kalpas, *sæcula*) of destruction, renovation, establishment, and decay. When the earth and the heavens are destroyed (the last destruction was by water, the next will be by fire), the whole face of nature is reduced to an abyss or chaos. From the face of the waters covering the wreck fresh forms are produced, and the world springs again into life, "another and the same."

But this part of my subject is so interesting that I shall translate somewhat in detail particulars relating to it.

First I will quote from the Avatamsaka Sûtra:—"The universe is not perfected by one influence or operation (*fiat*), but by many influences. For after the universe has been destroyed, and for a long time all has lain dark and void, there arises (through the *force* of the karma of all sentient existence) a wind which excites rain. The wind exciting the rain, there is a great ocean produced which extends throughout the universe. On this various winds begin to move; by these the several parts of the universe are perfected."

Next the Hi-shi Sûtra (Book of Creation, or Genesis) says:—"An incalculable time having elapsed after the complete destruction of the world, there arises a vast cumulous cloud which spreads itself abroad and broods above the heavens. From this there falls a fruitful rain, the drops as large as a chariot wheel. Through a hundred thousand myriad years the water from this rain gradually accumulates, until up to the very heavens it is spread out a mighty ocean. The 'four winds' hold it thus collected.[1] At length, after the cessation of the

[1] Ezek. xxxvii. 9.

rain, the waters having subsided countless *yojanas* in depth, a 'mighty wind' springs up, which, blowing on the face of the water, causes it to roll in tumultuous waves, from which a vast bubble is produced, which remains fixed, and from this the universe is framed."

At the beginning of the Sûtra known in China by the name *Chung-hu-mo-ho-ti*, which is probably another form of the Mahâvastu according to the Sammatiyas there is an account of the origin of the world on this wise:—Buddha has been requested by his followers to give an account of his previous history, *i.e.*, in former births, as to places, and circumstances, and family connections. To this he replies (K. i. fol. 1 *b*), addressing the congregation of Śâkyas (*i.e.*, disciples), "In former days I did not desire to enter on these particulars, lest the heretic followers of Mâra (or the Mâras and the heretics) should slander me and say, This Shaman Gotama speaks of himself things agreeable and pleasant, but things disagreeable and unpleasant he speaks not; what benefit is there in this?"

At this time the Great Mogalan[1] being among the great congregation, rising from his seat, looking at the face of Buddha, without removing his eyes, so remained. Then the Lord addressed Mogalan, "Those Sâkyas would gladly hear my past history, the places in which I have been born, of what family and clan, and under what circumstances. Consider then with yourself whether you consent or not to declare these things for their sakes."

At this time the Great Mogalan remained silently lost in thought. Then folding up his robe for a pillow, he lay down on his right side with his head supported by it, and thus lying as in sleep, he passed into a condition of trance[2] (samâdhi), and beheld passing before him the past history of the Lord, where he had been born, his family, clan, and circumstances of birth. Being thus enlightened as to every particular, he aroused himself from the trance and occupied his seat in the congregation as before. Then the Great Mogalan addressed the congre-

[1] Mu-lin, Ch.

[2] Compare Hugh Miller's account of the Mosaic vision, "Old Red Sandstone, p. 187.

gation of Sâkyas saying: "In my trance I beheld[1] the things that concern those Gotamas in times past. At the time of the destruction of the world, then the beings living in the world were born in the Suddha heaven, perfectly formed as to members, lovely to behold, without sorrow, with hearts full of happiness, every characteristic sign resplendent with glory, able to transport themselves through space, self-sufficient, able by tasting heavenly nectar to extend their lives, so that there were none who died in mid-age or when young. At this time the great ocean on the earth reached high up into space as a wide-spreading sea. Then the wind blowing on the water, a thin and unctuous substance like cream[2] was formed, which as it cooled became fit for the food of creatures hereafter to be born, a pure and unearthly substance to taste."

Agâin Mogalan, addressing the assembly, said: "At this time, during the age of destruction, 'all creatures' were born in the Subhakiṇho[3] heaven. Their term of years in this heaven coming to an end, they were born on earth. Their bodies remained as they had been in heaven, glorious in appearance, all their members perfect, their colour excellent, their forms ever resplendent, their years long in duration, their minds joyful and happy, perfectly self-sufficient, and able to move freely through space. At this time there was neither sun, nor moon, nor stars, nor periods of time, and no distinctions of sex. Born thus in the world, they desired to taste of the earth. Descending, therefore, they touched it with a finger and tasted it. Having thus gained a knowledge of its taste, they ceased not to partake of it till by degrees they lost their angelic beauty and splendour, and their spiritual faculty of instant locomotion, and became gross and coarse as men. After this a great black wind[4] arose, which blew upon the face of the waters, and produced the sun and the moon. These revolving round Mount Sumeru illuminated the earth (the four continents). On beholding them come forth men were filled with joy, but when they

[1] Kwan, *beheld in contemplation*, or *had revealed to me*. Compare as before Hugh Miller in the "Old Red Sandstone."

[2] Compare this account with "Manual of Buddhism," p. 64 *et seq.*

[3] "Extended purity," corresponding to the *Subhakṛtsna* of Burnouf, Introd., p. 613, and apparently with the *Subhakinho* of Childers' Dictionary, *sub voce*. Compare "Manual of Buddhism," p. 32 n.

[4] That is, "a tempestuous wind."

disappeared they were grieved. From this time forth began morning and evening, darkness and light, and the revolving seasons. Now at the time when the kalpa of renovation first began and men appeared (as we have described), there was no distinction of male or female, honourable or mean, but all were born alike in the world, and from this arose the expression 'all living things.'[1] But so it was, that those who tasted the earth frequently lost their personal beauty and became gross and dark-faced, whilst those who tasted it sparingly still retained their beauty and splendour of face. Hence sprang distinctions, such as excellence and inferiority, and from these came contentions about 'yes' or 'no.' Gradually the taste of the earth was exhausted, and then men began to be angry and full of anxiety. 'Alas! they said, what misery! the earth no longer retains its taste!' Then was produced a surface to the earth like a thin cake; after which, the surface being destroyed, there was produced a substance soft like flesh, which in its turn disappeared, and a rich loam was of itself generated, like the extract of the peach (or sugar-cane)."

Again he said: "The unctuous character of the earth no longer continuing, there was produced a double stem *p'u-t'au* plant,[2] whose taste was also sweet. For a long time eating this, the appearance of all (men) was pleasant and jovial. Afterwards, when this disappeared, there was produced a sort of dry powder like bran, without any glutinous qualities, and incapable of being sweetened, after eating which the sexes were developed. Moreover, there sprang up of itself an illicit sort of scented grain, which caused the bodies of those who ate it to become weak and degenerate, then the sexes were developed, and from this came the name of man and wife. Afterwards, when the lustful passion in different creatures continually increased, there was constituted the fixed relationship of marriage; and after this the Abhâsvara Devas came down and were born of women; and thus the race continued to be propagated. Then men began to build cities and towns, and the

---

[1] This phrase, "chung sing," is the one commonly used in Buddhist books to denote "all sentient creatures," or "all things that have breath."—(*Satta.*)

[2] The "p'u t'au," explained afterwards as being the same as the "lin t'ang," probably the "wild vine," or perhaps the "sugar-cane."

fruits of the earth which were gathered in the morning ripened again of themselves before the evening, and those gathered in the evening ripened before the morning."

Again he said: "The grain when four inches in length had no more reed;[1] men used to gather then as much as they required for the day; after this, they came to gather as much as they wanted for five days; then gradually the grain deteriorated, and when reaped did not grow again, but there sprung up in its place briars and weeds. At this time men were filled with anxiety and grief, so that they shed tears. Each one forthwith began to appropriate a certain amount of land to himself, in order to a fair distribution of the earth's fruits. After this, when they had learned to gather in and store their fruits, they began to pillage and rob each other's land, so that there was no safety, on which they determined to appoint one man as judge, who should protect the people on virtuous principles—rewarding the good, and punishing the bad, whom they agreed to support and enrich from the common stock. They therefore elected a man of commanding presence and conspicuous virtue, and this man they called their Lord. From this circumstance arose the title of people and king; he indeed, walking in the line of perfect virtue, protected the people as a father and a mother protect their child, and the people venerated him as the child venerates its father; the years of men were very many, and their happiness without bounds."

We find a similar account in Jin-ch'au, extracted from the Dirghâgama. It runs as follows: "At the time of the renovation of the world, the Abhâsvara Dêvas came down to the earth, each possessed of a shining body, flying as they went, and self-existent. Seeing the earth's crust was fragrant and sweet, they took it and ate it much. Then they lost their spiritual powers, their bodies became heavy and their brightness disappeared. The sun and the moon then began to be; and (because men coveted to eat) the richness of the earth came to an end. Then was produced the Po-lo plant; when this disappeared, there was produced a sort of fragrant rice (kang mai), in length four

[1] The text is here defective.

[2] *Fă-kiai-'an-lih-t'u.* *Vide* "Catena of Buddhist Scriptures."

inches, which being cut down in the morning, grew again before night. Nourished by this, the distinctions between male and female began to be exhibited, and men began to do things contrary to purity; this caused them to collect in families, and to become idle and listless, so that they began to think thus: 'It is much labour to gather food for each day's supply, come! let us gather enough for seven days, and store it up.' Then the grain, after being gathered in the morning, did not grow again. So men began to cultivate the ground and divide it in lots; whereupon they began to rob and pillage each other, and wars and fightings commenced. Then all men agreed to obey one man full of wisdom, called San-mo-to (Sammata), whom they made lord of the soil; all whom he blamed, they agreed to blame (or, whatever went wrong, they held him responsible), and whatever fruits the class of landowners obtained, they agreed to apportion a share of it to him as his right—hence sprang the caste of the Kshatriyas. Then, again, there were some men who left their homes and resorted to the mountains to seek wisdom, and to remove themselves from the influence of evil: these were called the caste of the Brahmans. Those who practised the arts of the artificer were called the caste of the Ku-sse (house lords), whilst those who laboured in the fields for their daily bread were called Sudras. From among these castes, men who used much consideration (*quiet* consideration), and, in view of the impurity of the world resulting from the sin of covetousness, resolved to forsake their home and become ascetics, these they called 'Shamans.'"

These extracts will be sufficient to show that in Buddhism we have preserved to us fragments of early traditions respecting the creation of the world and the origin of mankind, different from anything found in the Brahmanas. In fact, we are told[1] that "the Brahmanas presuppose a complete break in the primitive condition of the Aryan settlers in India. At the time when the law was laid down about the employment of certain hymns at certain parts of the sacrifice, the original meaning of these hymns, and the true conception of the gods to whom they were

[1] Ancient Sanscrit Literature, by Professor Max Müller, p. 429.

addressed, had been lost." So again, Dr. Muir says:[1] "When we descend from the hymns (*i.e.*, of the Vedas) to the Brahmanas, although we discover perpetual allusions to the earliest conception of Vishnu as traversing the sky in three strides, yet he no longer appears exclusively under that character but becomes invested with some new attributes, and forms the subject of various new legends which are quite foreign to the hymn; at the same time that he is still very different from the deity of the same name who is described in the Puránas." So again, Weber[2] assures us of "the posteriority of Manu to the whole body of Vedic literature."

We may regard, then, the fragments of truth we meet with in Buddhist records, as survivals from a primitive and independent stream of tradition.

But another interesting study in this matter is connected with a comparison of some Buddhist legends relating to the gods or demigods who occupy the zones or stages of Mount Sumeru, with the Homeric system of Olympus.

I have already pointed out that the "flowings of Ocean" which Homer names as surrounding the earth are known in the Buddhist myth as the "flowings of the Salt Sea" (*hien shui*) enveloping the four quarters of the world.

Within this sea is another—the Fragrant Ocean. This seems to correspond with the Erythræan Sea of the Greeks, which extended from Ethiopia to Taprobane; that is, from the coasts bordering on the Indus to Ceylon. Its name, the "Fragrant Sea," may be connected with the Fragrant Mountains of Gândhâra. Gândhâra was an ancient kingdom bordering on the Cabul river, and extending at one time from the spurs of the Hindu Kush to the lower streams of the Indus. The sea bordering on this region might well be called after its name, the "Fragrant Sea." There is a singular feature in this inquiry; by referring to the Buddhist Kosmic system, it will be seen that the outside circle of rocks separating the Fragrant Sea from the Salt Sea is called "the earth-holding mountains" (*chi-ti-shan*), and in the second Sermon of Asvaghosha, trans-

---

[1] J. R. A. S., vol. xx. part 1, p. 32.
[2] Hist. of Indian Lit., p. 277 (English edition).

lated in my third lecture, you will see that the Brahman disputers with the Upásaka connected Gândhâra with some "earth-holding" power. It seems probable, therefore, that Gândhâra was connected with these mountains, or a range of mountains so called, at an early date, and also with the Fragrant Sea, beyond which was the wide ocean surrounding the earth.

And now, following the ascending zones of Sumeru, which, according to the Buddhists, are ruled over by successive demigods, we have a marked agreement with the Homeric system. At the bottom of all, nearest the sea, is the god "Strong-hand" (*vṛisha-pâṇi*), which corresponds with the Greek Helios, the lowest of the minor deities in Homer. The word *vṛishan* has been thoroughly explained by Professor Max Müller;[1] it undoubtedly refers to the sun, as the *bull* or the *hero*.

Above this zone comes the demigod called "Chaplet-holder," which Burnouf has identified[2] with Sragdharâ or Âryatârâ, that is, "the stars" (*Sansc.* tára; *Zend*, stárĕ; *Greek*, *ἀστηρ*).

Above him comes "The ever-free," that is, the "Moon," or "The Wanderer;" or, under another aspect, "Soma," or "Liber," or "Dionysus."

At the crest and around the plateau of the Meru, we find four elemental gods, commonly known as the four kings, keeping the gates of heaven, and concerned in the affairs of men. These are, under one aspect, the Horæ of Homer; under another, the four elements. On the south, Virudhaka, the *productive* Earth (*ἄρουρα*, called by Homer *πολυφορβος*; as in the Chinese, *chang tsang* (the productive).) On the west is the large or distorted-eyed god (virûpâksha), corresponding with Air, represented under the form of the full moon, the queen of the night air. This title, *virûpâksha*, is in Chinese rendered "large eye;" corresponding with the ox-eyed or large-eyed Juno. The large eye is, in fact, the full moon rising in the east, or the forehead of the bull as the sun sets, and so Moschus in his Idyl[3] describes the bull that carried off the maid, thus—

[1] The Sixth Hymn of the First Book of the Rig Veda, J. R. A. S., vol. iii part 1, N. S. pp. 208, 209.

[2] Introd. to Ind. Budd., p. 542, and compare the whole account.

[3] Europa, l. 84 ss.

τοῦ δ' ἤτοι δὲ μέν ἄλλο δέμας ξανθόχροον ἔσχεν
Κύκλος δ' ἀργυφέος μέστῳ μάρμαιρε μετώπῳ.

This is typical of the moon at the full. And so we say the *bull's eye* for the central white circle of the target. And the ox-head sandal-wood (*gôsirsha chandana*) is sandal-wood with a white circle in the middle. And it is probable that the horse of Alexander, "Bucephalus," was so called from having a star or circle of white hair in his forehead, a mark, as Moschus tell us, contributing to the beauty of "the bull." We see, then, why Juno (*Πότνια 'Ηρη*, Queen of the Night) was called *Βοῶπις*.

On the north we have the element Fire, figured under the name Vaisravana, the son of Viśravas "the celebrated." Here is plainly the Hephæstus, the *περικλυτος* of Homer. He is described as *rich*, hence the same as Kuvera, as *lame* (and sometimes drawn without legs), and as *black*. How well this last epithet (Mahákála) represents the *black* unwashed Vulcan, as he was when Thetis sought his company on account of Achilles, we need not remark.

On the east is Dritarashtra, "he who holds his kingdom," *i.e.*, all-embracing *water*, the *γαιηόχος Ποσειδῶν* of Homer (Od., viii. 350).

Above all, and over all, is the Divine Śâkra, "the powerful;" the cloud-driver or cloud-compeller, or, as the Eastern writers put it, riding on his mighty *elephant* Airávata; this deity is described as having a palace on the very top of Meru (*ἀκροτατῃ κόρυφῃ*), whilst the gods, *'Ολυμπία δῶματ' ἔχοντες*, dwell around him. These gods are limited to thirty-three, which number, in all Northern Buddhist books, corresponds to "the year," "the four seasons," and the "twenty-eight days of the month."[1] The Brahmanas give another and distinct origin of the number.

One thing is plain; the system of the thirty-three gods and their heavens was known in the Vedic period; of that we are sure, for they are distinctly named;[2] and we also know that in Buddha's time the system of the Brahmalokas placed above the thirty-three heavens had been developed. We may reasonably

[1] Compare *Surângama Sûtra*, K. vi. fol. 8.
[2] *Vide* J. R. A. S., New Series, vol. i. part 1, pp. 60, 61.

suppose, therefore, that the period known in Indian literature as the Brâhmaṇa period corresponds with the time during which these superimposed heavens were invented: while the Vedic period embraces the period dating from the earliest worship of Helios or Savitri, up to the time of the settlement, so to speak, of the thirty-three gods on Meru. Buddha again, by a fresh departure, starting from the latest development of the Brâhmaṇa period, returns by "stemming the flood" to what was possibly the most primitive of all worship, viz., that of the first uncreated and uncreating principle, the eternal That, which "breathed breathless." So that, as at the bottom of this ascending scale we find the "strong-hand," *i.e.*, "the sun," worshipped, so at the very top we are brought back, by one who in himself embodies the characteristics of sun-worship, to supposed first principles, in themselves underlying all worship. Thus it is in this, as in all things human, the mind, baffled in the search after hidden truth, falls back upon itself and returns to its right position of confessed ignorance.

I said above that Buddha, or the legend of Buddha, embodies in it the characteristics of sun-worship. This has been well shown by M. Sénart in his "Legende du Buddha." But it is manifestly the case if we only consider the ordinary representations of Buddha's person. He is figured as in the diagram before you (*vide fly-title* of this lecture) in the character of the sun rising above the hills. His jewelled crest is called the *rasmi cúlámani*, that is, the ray-jewel-crest; and the Ceylonese figures of him are generally provided with his crown of triple rays. And so under various forms these rays are drawn till we come down to the figure of the trisul or *çudamani*, placed above the lotus, the analogue of the sun "rising from the water." Strange that at last, under the form of these triple rays thrice repeated, we discover the debased worship of Buddha as "the Lord of all that moves," in the Jagat-nátha of Purí!

The Essenes.

Whether the Essenes owed their rules of life to Buddhist influences in Palestine or not, the agreement of these rules with Buddhism is very remarkable. Nor is there any difficulty in supposing that a knowledge of Buddhism had reached so far as Judea, before Christ. It would be strange, considering the close intercourse between the Greek Bactrian kingdom and Syria, if it had not. Buddhism in India undoubtedly owed much to Greek art in Bactria; and the same workmen who were employed at Taxila, may have worked at Antioch. At least, there is no improbability in such a supposition.

At any rate, when the Greek Bactrian kingdom was overthrown, we may reasonably suppose that many of the colonists would return to lands nearer home, and seek intercourse with their brethren in Syria, and, perhaps, among the Macedonian colonists in Samaria.

The Greeks were supplanted by Parthians—and not only do we find Parthians Buddhists, but we read of Parthians among the Jews at Jerusalem keeping Pentecost.

We know not, indeed, how soon Buddhism acquired influence amongst the Parthian people—we only know that Buddhist missionaries from the Arsacidæ came to China at an early date after Christ; and that Kanishka, who was a Scyth, and constantly embroiled with the Parthians, was a Buddhist, and he lived at the beginning of our era.

But there is no need to urge this matter. My aim is simply to show that the agreement between Essenes and Buddhists may be accounted for in this way, without any prior improbability.

The following summary of Essene customs will serve us for all purposes of the present inquiry.

According to Josephus[1]—

1. The Essenes are a society of men friendly towards each other, holding marriage in no esteem, but yet not absolutely against it.

2. They hold riches in great contempt. Community of goods is maintained in a very admirable manner. No man can possess private property.

3. They look on it as a disparagement to make use of oil, and they always go habited in white garments.

4. They have stewards for the management of their affairs.

[1] Prideaux, Connection, book v. part 2, p. 268, fol. ed.

They give reception to all travellers of their sect. . . . They neither sell nor buy.

5. They are . . . in an especial manner religious. Before the sun be risen they speak of no common worldly matter, but till then offer up their prayers in ancient form, supplicating in them that he would make the sun to rise upon them. . . . They wash themselves, and being then purified they go into the refectory, . . . where, being set in silence, the baker puts before every man his loaf of bread. . . . The priest then says grace, . . . and after dinner they say grace again. No noise or tumult ever disorders the house where they are.

6. In offices of assistance and of mercy they are permitted to have free power.

7. They are great curbers of their passion, . . . and every word with them is of greater force than an oath with other men.

8. When any desire to enter their sect they are kept without a whole year, as novices, . . . to make trial of their continence.

9. Before they are admitted to eat at the common table, they solemnly bind themselves, &c.

10. Such as are guilty of any enormous crime they expel out of their society.

11. They are most exact and just in the administration of justice, never giving sentence but when there are at least a hundred present.

12. They distinguish themselves from all other Jews by abstaining from all manner of work on the Sabbath-day.

13. They are divided, according to the time they have been in their ascetic mode of life, into four classes.

14. They are contemners of adversity, . . . and laughed while under torments, &c.

15. They affirm, agreeable to the opinion of the Greeks, that for the souls of good men there is ordained a state of life in a region beyond the ocean.

16. There are some among the sect who take upon them to foretell things to come.

17. They hold that fate governs all things.

So far the testimony of Josephus. Philo, who wrote before Josephus, makes the following remarks :—

1. Among the Jews there are some whom they call Essæans; they have their name by reason of their piety, from the Greek word ὅσιος. They do not sacrifice any living thing. They mostly live in country villages, and avoid cities.

2. They do not treasure up either silver or gold. They make no arrows, darts, or swords, &c., or any other instruments whatever that are made use of in war.

3. Merchandising, trafficking, and navigation they never so much as dream of. They condemn the dominion of masters over servants as impious, and destructive of the laws of Nature.

4. About ethics or moral philosophy they are much conversant. . . . The seventh day is held holy by them, . . . and they go on that day to their synagogues, where they sit in order according *to their seniority in the society.*

5. They live together in sodalities, eating and drinking at the same common table; so they there provide entertainment for any of the fraternity who shall come thither to them from any other place.

Again Philo, speaking of the Therapeutæ, or contemplative sect of the Essæans, says:—

1. There are both Therapeutæ and Therapeutides (women), so called, not because they practise the art of physic, as is commonly so called, but because they cure the souls of men.

2. They divest themselves of all their worldly substance, . . . and flee from their homes, leaving their brothers, children, wives, parents, and all their kindred.

3. They choose to make their abode without the walls of cities, in gardens, villages, and lone country places, seeking solitude, not out of an affected hatred of mankind, but for the avoiding and the mixing with men of different manners.

4. Their houses are built in a very frugal and mean manner, being fitted only for two necessary things, to keep them from the heat of the sun in summer, and from the cold air in winter.

5. Each of them hath in his cottage a little chapel, which they call Semneum or Monasterium.

6. They pray twice in the day, that is, in the morning and in the evening; at the rising of the sun and the setting of the same.

7. They have among them the writings of some ancients. They compose songs and hymns in praise of God.

8. On the seventh day they sit down according to their seniority.[1] They eat only bread and drink only water.

9. They have only two garments, and universally exercise themselves in modesty.

And as a summary of their behaviour at their great festivals, we may observe from Philo—

That they have no servants to wait, but brothers of their own society; that they sit down in order and without noise; that they have no wine or flesh, but only water and bread, salt and hyssop.

Pliny's account of this sect is simply in confirmation of their temperance and chastity.

Prideaux observes that these Essenes could *not be Christians*, for they are spoken of as a sect of long standing in Egypt, and that they had hymns and writings of ancient date.

But, secondly, he observes that as they regarded the seventh day so rigorously, they must *have been Jews*, or of the Jewish religion.

With respect, however, to this we may remark that "the Buddhist Sabbath was a day of religious observance and celebration for laymen and priests, and occurred four times in every month. On these days religious laymen (i.e., *white-clothed men*)[2] dress in their best, and abstain from all trade and worldly amusements."[3]

There is no improbability in supposing that their name, which is either "Essenes" or "Essaioi," is derived from the word *Isi*, gen. *isino*, plural *isí* or *isayo*. The meaning of *isi* is a "saint" or "holy man," which meaning agrees with Philo's derivation from the Greek ὅσιος, a word probably connected with the same root.

The Magadhî or Prakrit *Isi* is the Sanscrit *Rishi*, and this, with the addition of Maha (making a compound *Mahesi*, *i.e.*, the Great Saint), was a not infrequent epithet of Buddha.

It is a mistake to suppose that because the name "*Buddha*"

---

[1] This they reckon according to the time of their admission into the society, and not according to their age. [This is strictly a rule of Buddhism.]

[2] In the Syrian monument discovered in China the Syrian Christian students are called *white-clothed*.

[3] *Vide* Childers' Pali Dict., *sub voce* "Uposatho."

is not met with in the West, that therefore the doctrines of Buddhism were not known.

"Buddha" is a term descriptive of the great teacher's character as "the enlightened one" (ὁ πεφωτισμενος), or "the awakened," and was no personal appellative.

Even on the stone-cut edicts of Aśoka this epithet occurs but once.

But as "the saint" or "great saint," he was not uncommonly known, and his followers were also described as "isayo" or "Ἰσί-(νοι)."[1]

Thus far for the general argument. We come now to consider particulars.

Josephus remarks "that the Essenes hold marriage in no esteem, but yet do not absolutely oppose it."

1. So the Upásakas (Buddhist laymen) were not forbidden to marry, but yet marriage was allowed only as a degree of holiness next below "entire continency."

2. "Riches held in contempt; community of goods maintained." This is a distinctive mark of the Buddhist lay-disciple. The great Aśoka gave all his goods to the Church, and encouraged the discipline of the Samgha, which required "all goods to be held in common." Besides which, there is no direction so frequently found in Buddhist writings as "the duty of self-sacrifice and charity."

3. "They make no use of oil." This is a literal order found in the Buddhist community.

4. "They go habited in white garments." The Upásakas throughout the Vinaya Pitaka are described as the "white-clad."[2]

5. They have stewards, &c. This is the duty of the Buddhist *Karmadâna*, who takes the general management of the secular affairs of the convent.

---

1 *Vide* Oldenberg in his *Vinaya Pitaka*, in which this title is given to Buddha. *Vide* Index, Cullavagga, p. 339; and Childers states (Pali Dict., *sub voce*), that "Buddhas and Arahás are called isi."

2 There is also a well-known image of a female, with a child on her knee, common among Chinese Buddhists, and also known in India, as it is mentioned by *I-Tsing* in his account of Indian temples, and which is described as the "*white-clad* Kwan-yin," because she grants the request of the female lay-disciples that they may have children.

6. "They give reception to all travellers of their sect, and neither sell nor buy." This also is literally the case with Buddhists, even to the present day, insomuch that their monasteries are still used as "places for hospitality, where food is given without any charge."

7. With respect to the prayers of the Essenes before sunrising and at sunset, this is a rule of their order, as we are expressly told by I-Tsing. And in Mr. Dickson's translation of the *Patimokkam*, we have the words given us which the Buddhists use at grace.

The rules of the Essenes respecting the age of the members, the existence of novices, and the cause of expulsion, are all perfectly Buddhist.

But this question has been discussed with such learning and candour elsewhere, that I should not presume to say a word upon it if were not for what follows.[1]

There are, scattered through Buddhist literature (of the Northern school, at least), several remarkable stories, or parables, parallel to some found in the Gospels. The woman offering the two mites, the parable of the tares in the field, the story of the Samaritan woman, are instances of what I mean.

If we accepted the theory that the Essenes were connected with Buddhism, this would be sufficient to account for the presence of these parallel records or notices in the books of Northern Buddhism. The intercourse of Bactrian Greeks or Hellenists with Syria, and probably Samaria, where Alexander the Great had left a Macedonian colony, would be sufficient to account for it. To me, indeed, it appears most singular that the saying of Christ with respect to the woman who anointed him for his burying—if she be the same who wept at his feet, as is generally supposed—should be verified under a somewhat different form in the record of the tender woman who wept at Buddha's feet at the time of his death. It would seem as

[1] *Vide* Dr. Lightfoot (Bishop of Durham), Epistles of St. Paul, Colossians and Philemon, Excursus i., ii., iii. In note 2, p. 394 *op. cit.*, Dr. Lightfoot refers the name Σαρμανοχηγὰς to an Indian word *Sramanákarja*, "teacher of the ascetics;" the second member of this compound word should be written *acharya;* the German method of writing *karja* for *charya* was doubtless the cause of the error. Sarmanácharya would not mean, however, "teacher of the ascetics," but simply "one practising or professing (the life of) a Sarmana."

though the story were adopted and perverted by the Buddhists.[1] So also with respect to the Samaritan woman; there are now before me *three* versions of a story bearing marked likeness to this narrative, in the Chinese Tripiṭaka. These stories were brought to China by missionaries (Buddhist missionaries, I mean) from the West, and there translated. Now, it seems to me not an unreasonable surmise that those people of Sychar who were "clothed in white" were Essenes. And if the Essenes were connected with Buddhists, the story might well have been carried away by some traveller or brother from a distant clime, and so become known in Parthia and North India. The version of this story which I am about to put before you, was translated into Chinese by a Parthian ('An-shi-ko) about the middle of the second century A.D.

In the third version which was made by a Upásaka (Buddhist layman, *white-clothed*) called *Chi Yau*, the particulars of the woman asking Ananda how he could beg water of her, a Mâtangî woman (low-caste woman), and Ananda's reply, are much more detailed; they are very curious. This version, however, is too long to translate here, and as it is nearly the same as that given by Burnouf in his "Introduction to Indian Buddhism," there is less need to do so.

After placing before you this translation, I will add two others relating to the woman offering her two mites, and so conclude.

Mo-Tang-Niu-King, the Mâtangî Woman.

Translated by 'An-shai-Ko, *a Doctor of the Law, during the after Han Dynasty.*

Thus I have heard. Buddha was residing at Sravastî (the country of She-wei), in the garden of the friend of the orphans. At this time Ananda, holding his alms-dish, went to beg some food. Having eaten, he went along the side of a stream, and seeing a woman on the water-side carrying (a pitcher) of water,

[1] This supposes, of course, that the copy of the Chinese Vinaya Piṭaka in which the account of this woman is found, was put together after the Christian era. May we refer this, and other books, to the council held under Kanishka?

and going (homewards), Ananda begged some drink from her.[1] Immediately she gave him some. The woman then followed Ananda to the place where he was dwelling. Returning home she told her mother, who was called Mâtangî (what had happened). Then she lay down on the ground to sleep, and as she so lay she wept aloud. The mother asked her daughter why she wept so, on which the girl said, "Mother! you wish me to marry, but I will not have the man. I saw a man by the water-side, who asked me to give him to drink, and I followed him, and found his name was Ananda. I want to marry that man. If, mother, you do not get him to marry me, I will have no other."

The mother going out asked respecting Ananda, and having found out that he was one of Buddha's principal disciples, she returned and told her daughter that Ananda was an attendant on Buddha, and could not be married to her. The girl, weeping, refused to eat or drink. "Mother!" she said, "you understand sorcery; go ask Ananda to come here to eat." Ananda coming back with the mother, the girl rejoiced exceedingly.

Then the mother spake thus to Ananda: "My daughter desires to become your wife, my lord." Ananda said, "My religion (rules) forbids me to contract marriage." Again she said, "My daughter, if she obtains not my lord as a husband, will kill herself." Ananda replied, "My master, Buddha, permits not men and women to associate." The mother going within told her daughter. "Ananda is unwilling to make you his wife. He says his religious rules do not permit him to marry." The daughter, with tears, addressed her mother and said, "Your power as a sorceress, can it do nothing?" The mother answered, "No power (religious power) in the world can prevail against the way of Buddha, or the way of a Rahat."

The Mâtangî girl said again, "Just shut the door fast, for my sake, so that he cannot get away. When the evening comes, he will accede to my request, and take me as his wife." The mother having closed the door by her sorcery enchanted Ananda, and as the evening came she spread out a sleeping-mat for him to lie upon. The girl then filled with joy began to

[1] In the other versions she asks here, "How is it you beg water of me, a Mâtangî (low-caste) woman.

decorate herself. But Ananda declined to lie down to sleep, on which the mother (by her art) caused fire to come from the ground in the midst of the doorway, and as she drew Ananda by his robes she said, "Unless you consent to wed my daughter I will cast you into the fire." And now Ananda reproached himself for having degraded himself thus as a Shaman, a disciple of Buddha.

Buddha, by his spiritual power, seeing the condition in which Ananda was placed (delivered him). Ananda, on returning to the presence of Buddha, said: "Yesterday, as I went a-begging by the roadside, I saw a woman, and asked of her a little water to drink, and then came back to this place. But this morning, a woman called Mâtangî came and asked me to go with her and take my food at her house. Having gone, she bound me fast, and would have me wed her daughter. I said, I hold the rules of Buddha, and I am not allowed to marry."

Meantime the girl, seeing Ananda about to leave the house, wept bitterly; her mother said, "They who belong to Buddha, cannot be captured by any art of mine; did I not tell thee so from the beginning?"[1]

And now the girl desisted not from tears, her mind fast bound by thoughts of Ananda. The next day, early, she herself went forth to seek to draw Ananda. Again, she saw him going to beg, and following him as he advanced, she looked first at his feet, then glanced on his face. Ananda, filled with shame, avoided her, but still she followed him, and rested not. Ananda then returned to where Buddha was; the woman stood beside the gate, and when Ananda came not forth again, she wept aloud, and went her way. Ananda, standing before Buddha, said, "To-day the Mâtangî woman once more followed me." Buddha made him call her to his presence. The girl facing him, he asked her, saying, "Why do you persist in following Ananda?" She said, "I heard Ananda was unwed; I too have no husband; I would have Ananda take me as a wife." Buddha addressed the girl, "Ananda is a Shaman, closely shaved; but you have comely locks upon your head; if you are willing to be shorn, then I will cause Ananda to espouse

[1] This paragraph appears to be out of order in the original.

you." The woman said, "Let my hair be shorn." Buddha replied, "Go home and ask your mother to cut off your hair, and then come back." The girl, going home, spake thus to her mother, "Mother, the man you could not get to wed me, Buddha declares shall marry me if I consent to have my hair shorn from my head." The mother answered, "My child, whom I have borne, keep, for my sake at least, your hair! Why would you marry this Shaman? in the land there are great and rich men, of these I will get for you a husband."

The girl said, "Living or dying, I must have Ananda, and his wife alone I'll be." The mother said, "Why bring such disgrace upon my tribe?" The girl replied, "The mother who loves me, ought to do that which would rejoice my heart." The mother, weeping the while, took down the shears (knife) and cut the hair from off her daughter's head. Then the girl returned to where Buddha was, and said, "I have shorn my head." Buddha replied, "You love Ananda, but what part of him?" The girl said, "I love Ananda's eyes! I love Ananda's nose! I love Ananda's mouth! I love Ananda's ears! I love Ananda's voice! I love Ananda's step!"

Buddha replied, "The eyes, how full of tears! the nose, how full of mucus! the mouth, how full of spittle! the ears, how full of defilement! the body, filled with offensive fluids, impure the powers of generation—and when, perhaps, a child is born, it comes to die, and lies forgotten, and then what tears! Is there much gain in this?"

The girl now stood, lost the while in thought. She thought of all the impurities that dwell within the body, and then her heart came right, and she attained the wisdom of a Rahat.

Buddha knowing the change, addressed the girl forthwith: "Rise! and go to Ananda, where he is." The girl, overcome with shame, hung down her head, and falling prostrate at Buddha's feet, she answered, "Truly, I am foolish and besotted, and being so, I followed after Ananda; but now my heart has opened, and like a lamp shining amid the darkness, or a fire brightly burning dispels the gloom, so is it with me; or like a shattered ship that reaches the shore, or like a blind man who obtains a guide, or like an old man who gets a staff, so has the power of Buddha's religion come to my help and opened my mind."

Then all the Bhikshus asked Buddha, "The mother of this woman is a sorceress, how is it that she has reached the condition of a Rahat?" Then Buddha answered, and said, "Are you wishful to hear the circumstances of this woman's history?" They said, "Gladly we would hear such instruction." Buddha said, "This Mâtangî woman for five hundred generations has been Ananda's wife; during all this time they have together striven, together desired to learn my precepts, and now they are brought together, and enlightened together as brother and sister."

Buddha having explained this, the Bhikshus hearing it, were all filled with joy.

The Story of the Woman and her Two Mites.

From Asvaghosha's Sermons, vol. iv. p. 15.

An Extract.

Subject.

Again: "A man who bestows charity, if he is actuated by a supreme principle of faith in giving even two mites, shall receive a return beyond calculation."

The Story.

I heard that there was once a lone woman who, having gone to the mountain called *Chau-ngan* (day-dull), beheld the men on the mountain holding a religious assembly called the Panchavarsha pârishat.[1] Then the woman, having begged some food in the crowd, beholding the priests, was filled with joy, and uttering her praises, said, "It is well, holy priests! but whilst others give precious things such as the ocean caves produce, I a poor (woman) have nothing to give." Having spoken thus and searched herself in vain for something to give, she recollected that some time before she had found in a dung-heap two mites (copper mites), so taking these forthwith she offered them as a gift to the priesthood in charity. At this time the president (Sthavira), who had arrived at the condition of a Rahat (the fruit of Rahatship), and so could read the

[1] That is, a quinqennial assembly.

motives (heart) of men, disregarding the rich gifts of others and beholding the deep principle of faith dwelling in the heart of this poor woman, and wishing the priesthood to esteem rightly her religious merit, not waiting to take up his *vina* (lute), with full voice burst forth with the following lines (religious cantos), as he raised his right hand and said, "Reverend priests, attend!" and then he proceeded:—

"The mighty earth and vast ocean,
Whatever treasures they contain,
According to this woman's intention
Are all bestowed in charity on the priesthood.
With careful mind and pious consideration,
Practising herself in the discharge of good works,
She has reached the goal of deliverance,
And utterly put away all covetous and selfish aims."

At this time the woman was mightily strengthened in her mind as she thought, "It is even as the Teacher says, what I do is as difficult as for him who gives up all his treasures;" and then, exulting in the act although sorrowing on account of her poverty, she prostrated herself before the priests and offered her two mites to the president, weeping as she did so and cast down in heart, and then she recited the following lines:—

"May I through all successive births
Escape such poverty as now afflicts me!
Enjoying for ever such happiness (as plenty brings),
With friends and relations in equal condition.
I now offer in charity priestly-fruit,
May Buddha rightly discern (my aim);
And as the result of this religious act,
May I soon obtain answer to my prayer.
The good and pious intention of my heart,
May it result soon in outward prosperity."

Then the woman having left the mountain, sat down beneath a tree, whilst a cloud canopy above her sheltered her without intermission from the sun.

Now at this time the king of the country, having just performed the funeral obsequies of the queen, was walking abroad to see the country, when observing the cloud canopy, he went to the tree over which it rested, and there seeing the woman, his mind was filled with desire. [He takes her to his palace and bestows upon her gifts, and places her in authority as his chief wife.]

Fo-shwo-A-che-sai-wang sheu-kiueh-King.

Buddha utters a prediction concerning Ajâtasatru Râja.

I have heard thus. On one occasion Buddha was dwelling in the country of Râjagriha in the Ghridrakûta (Ki-che-kiu) mount. At this time Ajâtasatru Râja asked Buddha to an entertainment (to dine). After the meal Buddha returned to the Jetavana.[1] The king, being then in consultation with Chi-pó (Jiva, *i.e.*, *Jivaka*), said, "To-day I asked Buddha to an entertainment, and he having eaten has gone back to his abode. What more should I do?" Jiva replied, "You should cause numberless lamps to be lighted."

On this the king ordered a hundred measures of oil to be taken from the royal gate to the Jetavana Vihára.

At this time there was an old woman who was very poor, but who had always entertained a supreme desire to make an offering to Buddha, but on account of her poverty had been unable to do so. And now observing what the king was doing, she was stirred up to effort, and going a-begging she got two mites given her in charity. Then going to an oil-shop she desired to buy two mites' worth of fat. The oil-master then addressed her thus: "Old mother, you appear to be very poor, and you have got there two mites by begging, why do you not buy some food with them for your good?" . . . . The woman (mother) said, "I understand that it is difficult to meet with a Buddha when born, even once in a hundred kalpas; and now I have been fortunate enough to meet with a Buddha born in the world, and yet have been unable to make any offering to him. Now, to-day, I saw the king gaining vast merit by his religious offerings; incited by this, a thought sprang up in my mind, although

[1] It would almost seem from this, that the inventor of this story thought that the Jetavana was close to Râjagriha. Perhaps, however, it is a misprint for Venuvana.

in truth I am poor, yet I desire to burn one lamp in honour of Buddha, and for the purpose of laying a foundation for a future birth (in happiness)."

On this the oil-master, overjoyed, gave her the two mites' worth of oil, wishing that she might obtain her end, as he dealt out fivefold the quantity.[1]

Whereupon the old woman, going to the place where Buddha was, lit her lamp in his presence, thinking meanwhile this will not burn out half the night, and then she vowed this vow: "If in after-ages I am to obtain supreme wisdom, and to be born as a Buddha, then this oil will burn all the night and not be exhausted." Then paying reverence to Buddha she departed.

Now the lamps lighted by the king soon went out and expired, and although there were servants sent to feed them, still they would not revive; but the lamp of the old woman, single as it was, exceeded in brilliancy the whole array of other lamps, and during the whole night the oil was not expended, nor did the lamp go out. At length, as morning came on, the old woman came back and made reverential worship, with her head prostrate and her hands clasped. She then stood aside. And now Buddha addressed Mu-lin (Mogalin) thus: "The sky is now brightening, you may put out the lamps." Mogalin, in obedience to the order, went to put out the lights one after the other, when, lo! he found them all extinguished, except this one lamp belonging to the old woman. After trying three times to put it out without success, he raised his Kasháya robe in order to use it as a fan to blow out the light. But the flame burnt brighter and brighter, and although he exercised his utmost power (spiritual power) to blow it out, burnt even more brilliantly till it lit up the heaven of Brahma, and was visible throughout the whole universe.

Then Buddha addressed Mogalin: "Stop! stop! this is the light of one who hereafter shall be a Buddha. No spiritual power of yours can extinguish it. This woman, during different births, extending through 180 myriads (kotis) of kalpas, has offered religious offerings to different Buddhas, and from a previous Buddha received a prediction in reference to her future

[1] This last clause is a doubtful translation.

condition; but having failed to offer up a sufficiency of religious offering to that Buddha, she now has been born poor and indigent. But now, after 3000 kalpas, her merit will be completed, and then she shall be born as a Buddha, and be called *Su-me-tang-kwong-fu-lai* (Sumeru prâbha dipa Tathâgata); and in the world where she is then born there shall be no sun or moon, but the bodies of the people shall be self-luminous, and in the houses the gems shall emit a perpetual brilliancy like the splendour of the Trāyastrinshas heaven."

The old woman, having heard this prediction, filled with joy, mounted into the air 180 fathoms from the earth, and then descending bowed her head before Buddha, and departed.

The king hearing of this, asked Jiva, saying, "I made all these religious preparations with a view to secure merit, and yet Buddha gave me no assurance of future eminence, but this woman, who has only lighted one lamp, has yet received an assurance? Why is this?"

Jiva answered and said, "Although the king has done much, yet your heart was not single as this woman's was, who fixed her mind on Buddha alone."

Again the king went to ask Buddha to stop a while at the palace. On this occasion the king specially enjoined all the garden attendants to gather at early morn all the best flowers, and to bring them in good time to the palace, to be given as an offering (to Buddha).

And now at dawn, Buddha having left the Jetavana, proceeding along the road gradually, and with a dignified mien, preached the law as he went for the good of the people, and so about midday arrived at the palace. Now it so happened that as he went a certain garden attendant, holding the flowers in his hand, came forth from the garden enclosure into the street, and there met Buddha face to face; and as he heard him preach the law in the midst of the high road his heart was entirely filled with joy, and forthwith he cast the flowers he held in his hand above the head of Buddha, where they remained fixed in space, as a crown over the head. On this Buddha immediately uttered a predictive assurance and said, "You who have made your religious offerings to ninety myriads of Buddhas" (or during the same number of kalpas of Buddha, but most probably the symbol used is an interpolation), "after 140 kalpas, shall become a Buddha, under the name of *kioh-fa* Tathâgata." Then the man, overjoyed, immediately raised his body in the air, and afterwards descending to the ground, made obeisance at the feet of Buddha. He then reflected thus: "The king is of a hasty temper, and last night he ordered us to observe religious abstinence, and then take the flowers to him to offer to Buddha, and now I have my own self thrown them into the air above the head of Buddha and they are gone; of a surety the king, if I go to him empty-handed, will slay me." So going on he returned home, and forthwith arranged the empty flower-vases outside his door, and then entering he told his wife as follows: "This morning I left without my food (fasting), and now the king will order me to be killed; be quick, I pray, and get me some food (or prepare me some food)." His wife, hearing what he said, was greatly frightened and said, "Why, then, is the king going to kill you?" And then he told his wife the whole transaction from beginning to end. The wife immediately going out, went to beneath the tortoise[1] for some food (or for something to prepare for food). Meanwhile the Divine Śâkra filled all the empty vases with heavenly flowers, and then when the good wife was returning with the food she beheld all the vases outside the door filled with flowers of such splendid hues as could not be equalled on earth. Forthwith she told her husband, who, going out and beholding them, knew at once that they were divine flowers. On this his heart was filled with joy, and without staying to eat he took the flowers and entered (the palace). Just then he met the king coming forth to escort Buddha on the road. The king, seeing the flowers so large and beautiful, such as are seldom seen in the world, immediately asked the gardener, saying, "There are in my garden, it appears, many such beautiful flowers as these, and you have never before brought them to me as offerings. You deserve to be killed for your wickedness, sirrah!"

The gardener said, "Your majesty, there are no such flowers as these in your garden; but your servant, early this morning

1 Does this refer to a cupboard shaped like a tortoise-shell, just as our own dish-covers?

taking some flowers from your garden in his hand, by chance encountered Buddha on the road, so unequalled in his appearance that my heart, overjoyed, led me to cast the flowers above him. Hereupon he uttered in my favour a predictive assurance, on which, knowing that you would kill me, I went home to get some food, when, after a moment or so, going out of my door, I saw all the empty flower-vases filled with these flowers. I knew they were of heavenly, and not of earthly growth. And now, O king! although I am of lowly origin, and in my present condition only fit to keep the royal gardens, forbidden even to pass the barrier which divides the palace precincts from the road; yet now having done so and received the predictive assurance, I know that hereafter I shall be born in heaven, and when in the presence of all the Buddhas (Buddhas of the ten quarters), then there will be no further hindrance, but I shall be able to roam along the road free and unforbidden. The king may kill me; I fear nothing."

The king, having heard that he had received a predictive assurance, was filled with trepidation; the very hair on his body stood erect; and he fell down prostrate and worshipped (the man?) as a sign of his repentance.

And now Buddha, having come to the palace and partaken of food, after repeating some sacred sentences (incantations) went away.

Again the king inquired of Jiva, "When I formerly invited Buddha to an entertainment the old woman received a predictive assurance, and now to-day, after seeking, as I have, the merit of religious conduct, the garden-keeper has received a predictive assurance. Why should I only be forgotten? my heart is indeed cast down, what more can I do to secure the reward of merit?"

Jiva replied, "Although your majesty has earnestly striven for days to obtain religious merit, yet you have only used for the purpose the wealth of the country, which has been exacted from the people by high-handed, cruel, and passionate tax-gatherers; you have therefore obtained hitherto no definite assurance. But now only afflict yourself, offer up your own substance, take your own necklaces, and jewels, and costly gems, and with them make a jewelled flower, and with your queen and heir-apparent, your hands closed in devout supplication, unitedly and with earnest intention offer up the gift to Buddha, he will then cause his brightness to be shed on the king, and you will obtain a predictive assurance."

Then the king, putting away from him all his savoury viands, from morning to night observed the rules of abstinence, and then, taking from his body costly jewels, he called together before daybreak his most cunning masters of art to make the jewelled flower.

Then the king, and the queen, and the heir-apparent all lent their hands to the work, and after ninety days it was fully completed. He then made preparations to proceed in state to the place where Buddha was, when lo! one of his ministers standing by said that he had heard that Buddha had gone before to Kusinagara and there attained Parinirvâna (*died*). The king, on hearing the news, was overpowered by grief; he wept piteously, and with broken accents exclaimed, "I have made with my own hands, and with the most earnest intention, this (jewelled) flower. Buddha, though he has attained Nirvâna, will receive my offering, and I will go to the Gridhrakûta mountain and there offer it before the throne of Buddha; the place will relieve (spread out and expand) my mind (thoughts)."

Then Jiva said, "That which is called Buddha is without a body and without Nirvâna, it is not eternally fixed, nor is it without destruction or without existence. He who is possessed of the highest self, he is able to see Buddha. Buddha, although he dwell in the world, can be seen by none but those possessed by this highest self. Mahârâja! most true is it, that though Buddha has attained Nirvâna, yet may you behold him!"

Forthwith he proceeded to the Gridhrakûta mountain, and there he beheld the form of Buddha (revealed to him), whilst, half-saddened and half-rejoicing, he worshipped on his face restraining his tears. Then spreading the sevenfold-precious gem flower before him, he cast it before Buddha; then the flower, fixing itself in the air, transformed itself into a perfect jewelled canopy and remained over Buddha. Then Buddha delivered to the king the following predictive assurance:—"After 80,000 kalpas, during a kalpa named *hi-kwan*, the king shall be born as a Buddha called *Tsing-ki-sho-pou* Tathâgata, his domain (*t'sa tu*) shall be called *Fă-wang*. Then human life shall reach forty little kalpas." The king's eldest son, called *Chandavali*, was then eight years old. He, seeing his father receiving this predictive assurance, was filled with exceeding joy, and forthwith taking off his jewels he scattered them before Buddha and said, "Oh that I may be a golden-wheel king at the time when that *Tsing-ki-sho-pou* is born as Buddha, and may be privileged to make to him religious offerings; and, after his Nirvâna, may I be privileged to offer above his relics garlands and canopies."

Buddha answered, "It shall be even as you desire; at the time of that Buddha you shall be a golden-wheel king, and after your years are ended you shall be born in the Tusita heavens, and at the expiration of your term of life there you shall descend as a Buddha and dwell in the domain (*t'sa tu*) called *Luh-wong*, and receive the name of *Chandana*. Then the years of man's life shall be the same as during the time of the Buddha called *Tsing-ki-sho-pou*."

Having received these predictive assurances, the king and Chandavali, bowing before Buddha, lo! he disappeared amidst a blaze of glory.

The Sûtra called *Fo-shwo-a-che-sai-wang-sheu-kioue.*

[This is a specimen of the character of the later expanded class of Buddhist Sûtras.]

INDEX.

T.

PLATE I.

MOUNT SUMERU.

PLATE II.

THE FOUR KINGS.

PLATE III.

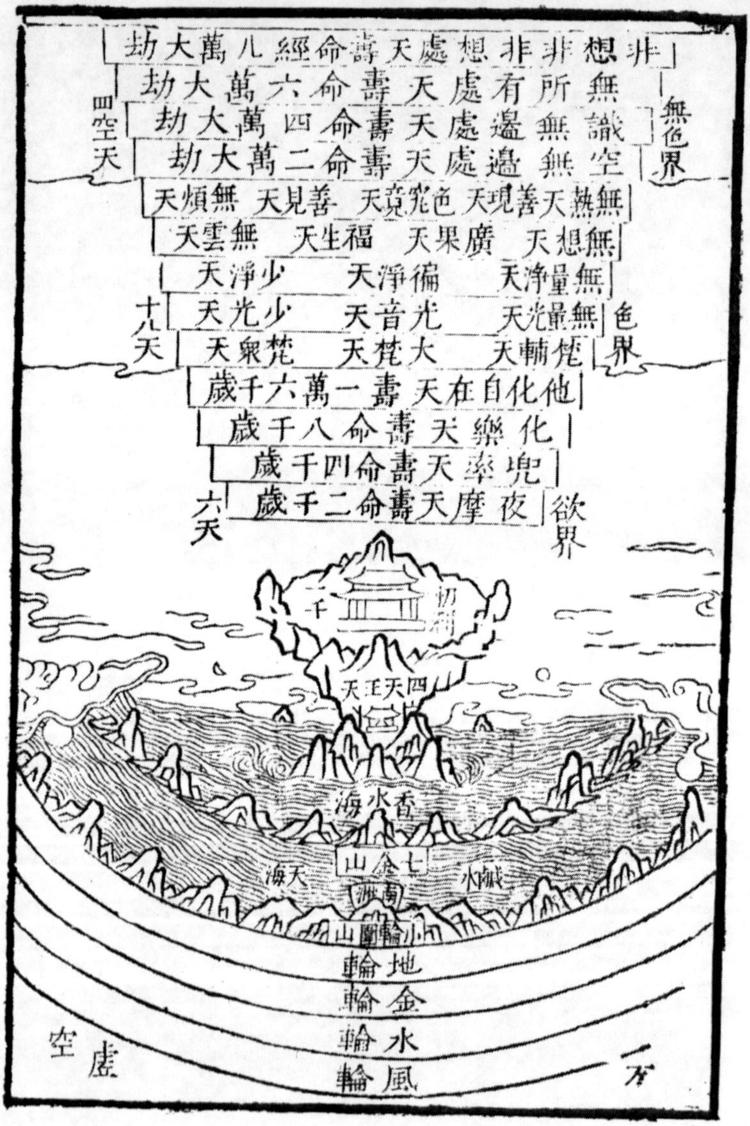

THE SAKWALA.

PLATE IV.

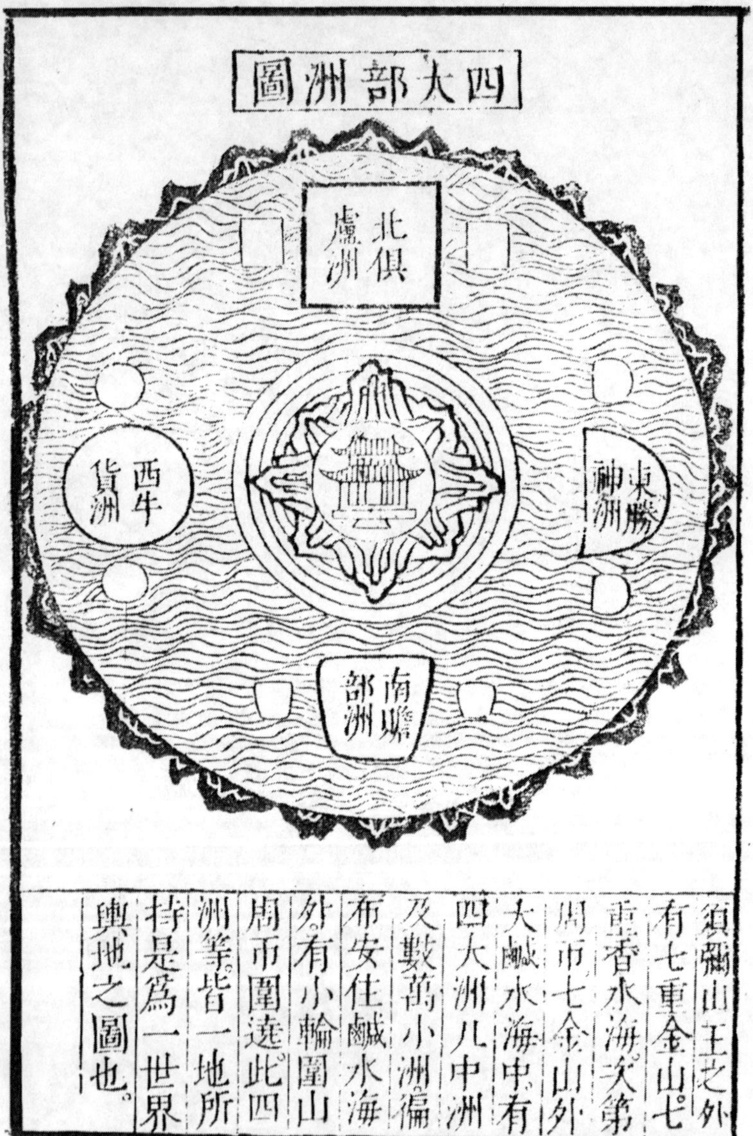

THE FOUR DVIPAS.

三十三天名出正法念處經

PLATE V.

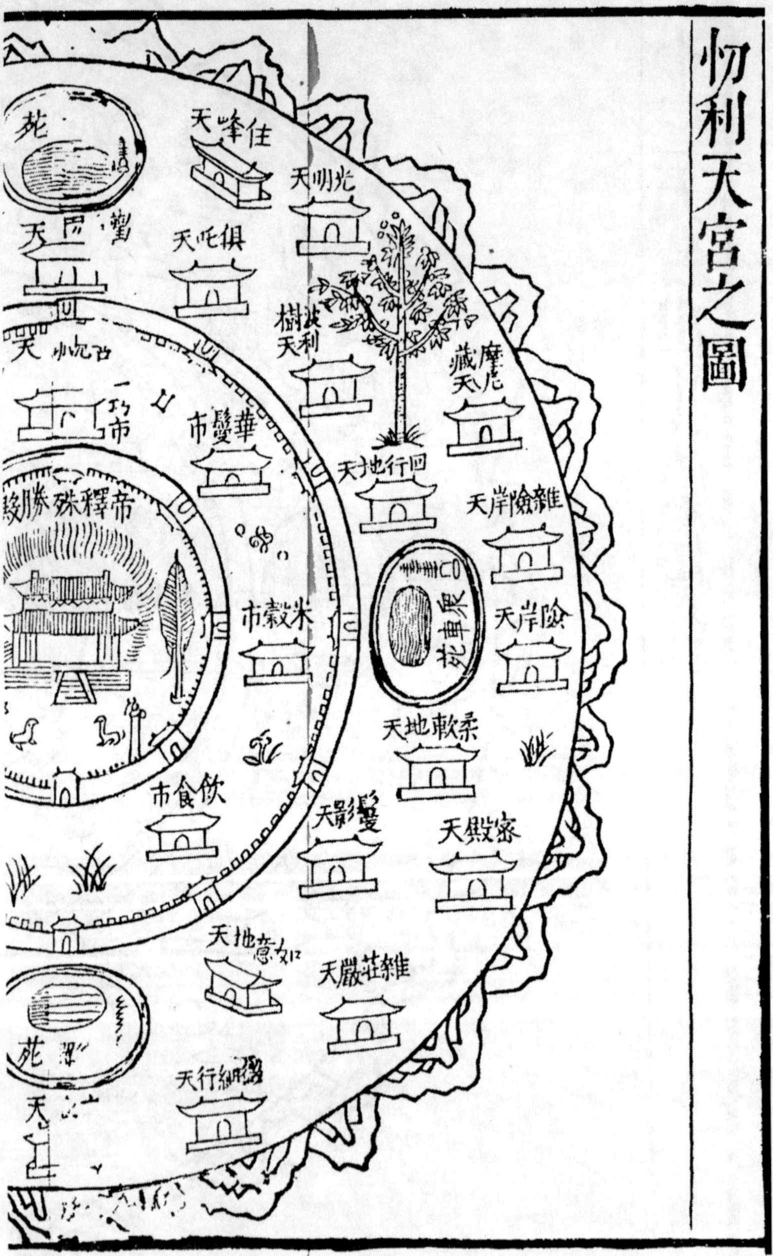

HIRTY-THREE GODS.